3ᵒᵒ
LPC

Future Hope:
A Winning Strategy for a Just Society

Ted Glick

A Future Hope Publications Book

ISBN # 0-87810-045-8

Future Hope Publications
P.O. Box 1132
Bloomfield, N.J. 07003
futurehopeTG@aol.com

Acknowledgments

This book is in large part the result of discussion and experiences with literally thousands of people over the years that I have been an activist for social change. I have particularly benefited from interactions over the last 25 years with people committed to building a new political party in this country. You'all know who you are.

Four people were especially helpful in giving me input and feedback over the several years that this manuscript was taking shape: Greta Gaard, Wayne Glick, Dave Jette and Victor Wallis.

Without the inspiration by example of my parents, Wayne and Barbara Glick, and the love and support of Jane Califf, my wife of over 20 years, and Daniel Califf-Glick, my son for over 16, this book would never have been written.

However, I am ultimately responsible for what is written in these pages. I hope that those reading it find it of value. I always welcome feedback and constructive criticism.

TABLE OF CONTENTS

OUR AWESOME TASK
May 6, 1997

I cried
for a long time
while driving
from Decatur to St. Louis,
   Monday,
     after Summit/97,
     on the way home
     to Brooklyn.

I cried
thinking about,
   feeling,
the power of
the weekend past,
but still
so many rivers to cross,
so many people
suffering and struggling
   unnecessarily,
   consistently,
   wrongfully,
in this world of pain.

I cried
thinking about
the children—
   the innocent,
   beautiful children,
   starving, abused,
   homeless,
   miseducated, hopeless,
   futureless—
the world over,
   UNLESS
   WE
   SUCCEED
in the awesome task
we have assigned
to ourselves.

I cried
because,
despite the power
of the weekend past,
we are powerless,
   right now,
   and for years
   to come,
   realistically,
   tragically,
to stop their pain.

I cried,
   I cried,
     I cried.

Where do we look
for strength
in times like these—
    hard times,
    struggling times,
    fighting-seemingly-
    insurmountable-odds
    times?

To one another,
as we learn
the "to (one another)
and not the "on"
that has been
our history
on the Left,
within the union structures,
in our other organized efforts—
    the competition,
    the pettiness,
    the backstabbing,
    the dishonesty—
a history that must be,
and fortunately is,
being transcended.

Progress was made
in Decatur.

Some find strength
in spiritual traditions,
    even rituals,
connecting us
    to one another,
    to those before,
    to the natural world.

Some love and meditate
on "God"—
    Truth,
    Justice,
    Compassion
    ("And what does God
    require of you
    but to do justice,
    and to love kindness,
    and to walk humbly
    with your God?")—
with all their heart
and soul,
and their neighbors
as themselves,
    fulfilling
    Humankind's
    Greatest
    Commandment.

Some gather children,
    grandchildren,
    neighbor children,
    friend's children,
    students,
around them—
    "and the little
    children
    shall lead them."

And some of us
just muddle along,
doing the best we can,
learning from history,
understanding
the historical truth,
the law of physics,
that for every action
there is a reaction—
that oppression
breeds resistance—
that,
as Dr. King said,
"The arc
of the universe
is long,
but it bends
toward justice."

Accepting—
we have no choice!—
our limitations,
our limited power,
    right now,
while never accepting
injustice and evil,
the evil system
we must transform;

Using our anger,
our outrage,
our humanity,
our love,
burning like
a low flame,
    a pilot light,
flaring up
as necessary
into a burning torch
to lead others
into a future,
    a future world,
we must,
    we have to,
        claim
            and
                win.

An Introduction

Future Hope is based upon research and writing that I did between 1993 and 1997, but more fundamentally it is based upon my thirty-two years of political activism. My activism began while I was in college in Grinnell, Iowa in the late 1960s. The Vietnam war and domestic racism were the two front-page issues which forced me to confront my life back then. This led to a decision to leave college after my second year in May of 1969 and to become a full-time activist against the war and for justice at home.

Since that time I have been involved in a cross-section of actions, organizations, causes and campaigns.

-Until 1973, my major work after leaving college was as part of the draft resistance movement. This included participation in a number of "actions," as we called them, in which Selective Service draft board offices, war-connected corporate headquarters and bomb-producing plants were non-violently disrupted. I spent close to a year in prison for a raid on a federal building in Rochester, N.Y., and I was indicted while in prison as one of the Harrisburg 8, falsely accused of a conspiracy to kidnap Henry Kissinger and blow up heating tunnels under government buildings in Washington, D.C. Those charges were eventually dropped.

-In the fall of 1974 I helped to found and then was a national coordinator of the National Campaign to Impeach Nixon, the most short-lived and successful organization in which I have ever participated.

-While working to get Nixon out of office, I met a number of people who were working to form a broadly-based, independent political party. I had come to believe that such an organization was essential if fundamental change was ever to come to this country, and I began to work actively with the National Interim Committee for a Mass Party of the People.

-As a leader in the Mass Party group I participated in unsuccessful efforts in 1976 by the National Black Political Assembly to recruit an African American independent Presidential candidate. I was also actively involved in a multi-racial and multi-issue July 4th Coalition which organized a massive, 50,000-person demonstration in Philadelphia on the Bicentennial of this country's founding.

-Out of the July 4th Coalition emerged the People's Alliance, whose major success was a People's Convention in August, 1980 of thousands of people on the devastated rubble of Charlotte Street in the South Bronx, N.Y., followed by a march of 15,000 people to Madison Square Garden on the first day of the Democratic National Convention. I was national coordinator of the Alliance.

-In 1983, out of what remained of the Alliance, I helped to form the National Committee for Independent Action (NCIPA). NCIPA's primary work for its first five-six years was to build the '84 and '88 Jesse Jackson for President campaigns and the National Rainbow Coalition. We believed that this African American-led effort had a realistic potential to become, over time, the kind of independent political party we were committed to. Unfortunately and tragically, following his 1988 Presidential campaign, Rev. Jackson decided that the advancement of his political career within the Democratic Party was more important than building the movement he had done so much to create. He proceeded to alter the Rainbow so that it became little more than a hollow shell of what it was in the process of becoming, a genuinely multi-racial, multi-issue, mass-based, independent political force. It was time to look elsewhere for that still-needed force.

-In 1990 I was part of a slate of four statewide candidates that unsuccessfully attempted to get a new Unity Party on the ballot in New York. In 1991 I was an independent candidate in a special City Council election in Brooklyn, receiving about 5% of the vote in a nine-person field. In 1992 I worked with former National Rainbow Coalition Executive Director Ron Daniels and others to organize a successful Peoples Progressive Convention in Ypsilanti, Michigan, out of which emerged an on-going National Peoples Progressive Network. All of this time I was the National Coordinator of NCIPA.

-I was also actively involved with community organizations in Brooklyn from the late '70s to the late '90s, working with tenants needing repairs or facing landlord harassment, organizing tenant associations, working on issues of unemployment, police brutality and racism, and co-chairing a community coalition that fought for neighborhood-oriented, and not big business, development on a huge plot of vacant land close to where I lived at that time.

-From 1988-1999 I was an adult counselor for the Future Leaders Network. Over the course of its existence the Future Leaders Network brought together 250 or more young people from around the country to Summer Institutes and other gatherings to discuss social and political issues and teach organizing skills.

-In 1992 I participated in a 42-day fast from September 1 to October 12 in protest against the official celebrations of Christopher Columbus arriving in the Americas. Since then I have helped to coordinate a national Peoples Fast for Justice network made up of people who fast between October 1st and 12th and organize local actions each year calling for freedom for political prisoner Leonard Peltier and the renaming of October 12th, Indigenous Peoples Day.

-For the past five years, however, my primary work has been as the national coordinator of the Independent Progressive Politics Network. This group emerged in 1995 out of a joint collaboration between NCIPA and the National Peoples Progressive Network. We felt it was urgent that we put together a stronger organizational vehicle to unify those of us on the Left who were clear on the need for an alternative to the Democrats and Republicans. Over the last four years we have held four national conferences, brought together close to 130 independent candidates from around the country onto a National Slate of Independent Progressive Candidates, participated in the efforts which led to Ralph Nader running as an independent for President in 1996, and undertaken other work to strengthen the independent progressive party movement. We have pulled together an impressive national network, multi-racial, broadly-based and getting broader, activist, growing and hopeful. I am especially pleased by the fact that the IPPN has developed a way of working that embodies the new culture, the new society we are committed to bringing into being.

What was my purpose in writing this book? The first purpose was entirely personal: to clarify my thinking about what I have learned over these past thirty years of activism, what I believe is necessary if future generations are to see a different country and a different world. Indeed, I am convinced that unless we succeed in "our awesome task" of transforming this society in fundamental ways, there may not be a future worth living in.

The times are urgent; to have hope for the future, we need a winning strategy for a just society, and we need to come together now to create the political movement, organizations and alliances that will make that strategy real. I pray that this book is of value in this crucial set of objectives.

LOVE AND SOCIALISM

Down through history, women and men of vision have worked to understand the societies in which they live so that they could make their maximum contribution to the process of changing them for the better. Some of these social change agents, these revolutionaries, have been motivated by religious beliefs and ideals. Others have been pushed onto this road by the conditions of their lives, by suffering, oppression, injustice and deprivation and a burning desire to get out from under them. Still others have engaged in serious study and reflection, leading to consciously developed historical/social/economic analyses as a basis for projections of new possibilities in the future, and as a guide to action to get to that future. Some have been motivated by all three.

Today, as we approach the beginning of a new millennium, there is a desperate need for this type of person, for human beings who take seriously their responsibilities to themselves and to others. People are needed who will work and study, alone and with others, for a clear and accurate understanding of our society, advanced industrial/technological society, and who will make a commitment to being an active part of the process of changing it for the better.

Any honest student of society must admit that humankind is in a perilous condition today. We live in a world dominated by a tiny corporate elite whose primary purpose is to amass ever greater fortunes for themselves no matter who or what, people, animals or the natural environment, gets hurt or destroyed in the process.

Because of this fundamentally, grossly and obscenely unjust set of realities, the entire world is in deep turmoil. We are confronted with increasing and potentially apocalyptic environmental degradation and the continuing danger posed by nuclear power and weaponry. It is a realistic possibility that our natural environment will soon reach a point of no return after which serious environmental disruptions, if not breakdowns, will become a way of life for those living on the earth.

There are periodic, massive famines in parts of Africa and Asia and the threat of famine elsewhere, and a rapidly accelerating gap between the poor and the rich both internationally and in the United States. Under our present global system, the financial assets of 358 billionaires is equal to the annual income of 2.5 billion of the world's poorest people. (1) The richest 20% receives almost 85% of the world's income while the poorest

60% try to survive on less than 6%. (2)

According to OXFAM, every day over 50,000 people, 2/3 of them babies and small children, die from hunger and related afflictions. There is the growing scourge of AIDS and the reappearance of diseases like cholera and tuberculosis in countries that have not seen such diseases for decades. One out of every four people in the world does not have access to safe drinking water. And the list can go on.

I believe that anyone who is genuinely concerned about the situation we are faced with in this country and world today needs to learn from the experiences of prior efforts to transform society in fundamental ways. The solutions to environmental degradation, continuing racism and sexism, widespread poverty, the growing gap between the obscenely rich and almost everybody else, a militarized economy despite the ending of the Cold War, homelessness, and all of the other problems facing us will not be found in half-measures. We can only begin to address these issues if we win control of our government from the corporate elite that now dominates both political parties and, as a result, government at virtually every level.

This presents us with a problem. We know from historical experience that the most noble of causes can turn sour, turn into its opposite, become a force of oppression rather than liberation. Individuals who once gave of themselves in heroic proportions can become hollow shells of their former selves, not to mention what can happen to once-revolutionary organizations. The difficulties faced by those who have come to power as a result of their commitment to social and economic justice have led many down the path of corruption in pursuit of personal power, wealth and privileges, or both.

Those who are grounded in religious traditions have an easy answer for the roots of this problem: sin, personal rebellion against God, a forgetting of the nearly universal religious command to love one's neighbor as yourself.

There is truth to this answer. Ultimately, we are each responsible to our own conscience, to the voice of "God", to a higher calling. Those who have provided the inspiration by example and the teachings which have led to full-blown religions were right to call us to account before the Great Spirit, what I like to call The Great, Unknown Creative Force in the Universe.

However, individual change alone, even individual change and righteous conduct joined with others within a spiritually-based organization--a church, a synagogue, a mosque, or some other form of religious community--is not going to change the unjust and destructive economic/political/social realities of 21st century U.S. society.

A political movement, one which learns from the experiences of past political movements, is an absolute necessity.

One great lesson is the necessity of integrating ethical and moral principles into our work. This is where those of us who see ourselves as spiritually-grounded individuals have a particular contribution to make. We have learned, or are learning, that it is not enough to say that we believe in justice and the truth; we must work to live out such principles in our lives, in the ways we relate to those we come into contact with on a daily basis.

This ethical commitment and development of a process for sustaining it was not made, by and large, within the traditional Marxist movement, at least not in an explicit and conscious manner. This is part of the reason why, once some of those movements came to power, in the Soviet Union, China and elsewhere, they became something other than what they intended to become. It is not the only reason, and probably not the main one; the main reasons are rooted in decades of exploitation and underdevelopment and the efforts of capitalist powers to destroy the feeble shoots of alternatives to capitalism by any means necessary. Those difficult "material conditions" within which revolutionaries attempted to radically transform society unquestionably were the primary impediment to the process of changing economic, social and human relationships.

However, using these realities as an excuse for the failures of socialism is like blaming old age for the fact that all people eventually die. Like old age, big business capitalism, for as long as it continues to exist on the earth, will always do whatever it can to cause the death of, to subvert and destroy, its historic rival, socialism. After all, socialism intends to put capitalism "out of business."*

---

*By socialism, I mean a political/economic/social system in which the needs of society are advanced through a process of public ownership and democratic control of the major industrial, financial and other institutions, rational planning as to what those institutions produce, and a just distribution of the products so as to consciously benefit all members of society.

Those of us who are interested in the truth of history must be much more rigorous about the <u>internal</u> weaknesses that were also responsible for the demise of the Soviet Union, for the tremendous inroads capitalism has made in China and the weakness of other socialist efforts elsewhere in the world.

The roots of this problem go back very far, indeed, back to Marx himself.

Without question Karl Marx was a humanist, a person who imagined an entirely different kind of society, one based on the principle, "from each according to their ability, to each according to their need." This is the complete antithesis of the principle of today's society: "from each according to their ability, to each according to whatever they can get away with." Seen in the light of the last 150 years of human history, since Marx began writing and publishing, Marx's vision is a profoundly idealistic, even utopian vision of the future.

Yet Marx was a hard-liner when it came to those who held high the necessity of moral reform in the society of that time.

Consider this statement of Marx' in <u>The German Ideology</u>, as quoted in Cornel West's <u>The Ethical Dimensions of Marxist Thought.</u>

"Communism is quite incomprehensible to our saint [referring to philosopher Max Stirner] because the communists do not oppose egoism to selflessness or selflessness to egoism, nor do they express this contradiction theoretically either in its sentimental or its highflown ideological form; they rather demonstrate its material source, with which it disappears of itself. The communists do not preach morality at all. . . They do not put to people the moral demand: love one another, do not be egoists, etc; on the contrary, they are very well aware that egoism, just as much as selflessness, is in definite circumstances a necessary form of the self-assertion of individuals." (3)

In this polemic Marx was arguing against a position of certain philosophers in his day which detached the individual from the historic, class and social context in which s/he was brought up and lived. He was objecting to an essentially elitist point of view which blamed individuals for problems which were primarily the result of unjust and oppressive social relations. Although this criticism is sound, as far as it goes, Marx had a real blindspot when it came to the connection between societal change and personal change. He didn't identify it as a problem to be grappled with, and he therefore made no attempt to address, much less answer it.

John Marsden, author of <u>Marxism and Christian Utopianism</u>, addresses this weakness in what Marx wrote and didn't write: "Marx far too readily talked of the 'mere fragment of a man' becoming the 'fully developed individual,' without attempting to bridge the chasm between the two. Jack Lindsay's comments in his discussion of Gramsci are particularly apposite: 'The transition to socialism needed the construction of a new common sense (good sense), a new culture in all spheres, a new philosophy, a new consciousness.'" (4)

In all fairness, it must be said that revolutionaries following Marx did have some appreciation of this critical need for a change in consciousness. Both the Soviet and the Chinese revolutions made deliberate efforts to bring about "cultural revolutions" within their respective societies, but both ultimately failed, in part because of the continuing hold of pre-revolutionary ideas and consciousness on both the leadership and the population as a whole.

Today in the United States there are possibilities for building a very different kind of political movement for fundamental social change, one which learns from this history and these experiences. One reason is the advanced level of industry and technology in the USA. This is a wealthy society (wealthy, it must be said, in large part because of slavery and the exploitation by huge corporations of the resources and peoples of Africa, Latin America, Asia and elsewhere, not to mention the Indigenous peoples and Mexicans whose land was taken from them here in North America.) This wealth <u>could</u> be used to create a new type of society, a society which could move relatively rapidly toward a much more just and egalitarian distribution of resources and much healthier social and economic relationships based on cooperation instead of individualistic competition.

But it is not just the economic development of our capitalist society that makes a transition to a new form of society possible. It is also the cultural transformations that have taken place over the past 50 or so years. Advanced capitalism has led to literacy and education on a mass scale. Women have been brought out of the home and into the job market, a major impetus for the women's movement which has emerged over the past 30 years. Increased social and geographic mobility, the opportunities for travel, as well as extensive mass communications, expose people to other ideas and cultures which, in turn, can broaden individual consciousness.

With this education and exposure comes an interest in and an ability to think about issues other than where the next meal is going to come from--something that was <u>not</u> the case for either Russia or China, heavily peasant societies. In a society such as ours, large portions of the working population are concerned about education, personal change and/or spiritual development. Psychologists and therapists were few and far between in Russia and China.

This reality opens up a potential, a necessity really, for positive cultural transformation on a large scale that a political movement serious about fundamental change cannot overlook.

This cultural transformation process must be an integral part of a new political movement in this country. Concretely, this means that a new movement must learn from the best of the women's movement and reject the competitive, hierarchical and self-centered styles of leadership that far too many men and some, mainly white middle- and upper-class, women often display. We need to learn how to work in a collective and cooperative way, a way which is distinctly different than the aggressive, me-first culture that is dominant in U.S. society today. We need to show by example, by the way the movement functions, that we have grown and learned beyond the old, destructive patterns of personal interaction. When one of us has a serious personal problem, an injury, an illness, a death in the family, or emotional distress, others must be there to provide support and assistance. We must be known not just for our good ideas about how to re-make society and our work on issues but by the way we interact with each other and with other people on personal levels.

Rosa Luxemburg, a Polish woman who was one of the leading European revolutionaries of the first 20 years of the 20th century, had some very appropriate words to say about this critical need:

"Unrelenting revolutionary activity, coupled with a boundless humanity--that alone is the real life-giving force of socialism. A world must be overturned, but every tear that has flowed and might have been wiped away is an indictment, and a man hurrying to perform a great deed who steps on even a worm out of unfeeling carelessness commits a crime." (5)

And more recently, in 1965, Latin American revolutionary Che Guevera put it like this:

"At the risk of seeming ridiculous, let me say that the true revolutionary is guided by a great feeling of love. It is impossible to think of a genuine revolutionary lacking this quality. . . We must strive every day so that this love of living humanity will be transformed into actual deeds, into acts that serve as examples, as a moving force." (6)

Our country and our world are on a collision course with nature and with ourselves. To alter this suicidal course, to build a new type of truly democratic and just society which can bring ourselves into harmony with one another and the natural environment, we need to build a new, people-oriented revolutionary movement, one based on Higher Love. This movement must organically combine positive personal change, and a culture which supports it, with effective political activism for societal change. It must do so by the development of an ideology, strategy and tactics appropriate for the 21st century, for the new millennium, building upon past ideologies, strategies and tactics but not chained to them. To maintain hope for the future, we need a winning strategy for these urgent times.

Footnotes

1) Barnet and Cavanaugh, Global Dreams: Imperial Corporations and the New World Order

2) U.N. Human Development Report, 1992

3) Karl Marx, The German Ideology, as quoted in The Ethical Dimensions of Marxist Thought, by Cornel West, Monthly Review Press, p. 81

4) John Marsden, Marxian and Christian Utopianism, Monthly Review Press, p. 177

5) Rosa Luxemburg, Rote Fahne, December, 1918, as quoted in Rosa Luxemburg, by Paul Frolich, Monthly Review Press, p. 189

6) Che Guevera, Socialism and Man, Pathfinder Press, p. 20

THE DANGERS OF REFORMISM
(NOT REFORMS)

In determining strategy, we need to be clear that we are not talking about half-measures, limited objectives, reforms that do not fundamentally alter the structures of oppression and exploitation, the domination of economic life and government by a tiny corporate elite.

The changes we are talking about, the changes <u>absolutely necessary</u> if humankind is to have a future worth living in and for, <u>must be</u> a process of liberation, a process of freeing individuals, institutions and the society as a whole from <u>old</u> patterns of thinking and acting and toward new ways of working with and relating to one another. It is not something which happens in a short period of time. It involves years, decades of maturation and development.

Yet there is one overriding, <u>specific</u>, collective act which must take place if the chains of oppression are to be broken to allow the full flowering of the liberating impulse: the present corporate class which dominates government must be removed from power, and a popular alliance representing the broad working class and much of the middle class, the vast majority of the population, takes control. Without this revolutionary act, without the elimination of the corporate class as a <u>ruling</u> class, there is no hope of fundamental social and economic transformation.

Not everyone who sees him- or herself as a revolutionary, a social change agent, a socialist sees things this way. Down through history, some have opted for a <u>reformist</u> course of action. What is meant by this?

Reformism has deep roots within the socialist movement. One of the most famous early reformists was Germany's Edward Bernstein. He consistently articulated the theory that the goal of socialism was not the conquest of political power but, instead, a long, drawn-out process of legislative reforms. This would be done within capitalism's legal framework and without the perspective of the need to directly challenge the ownership of the means of production and distribution by the property-owning elite. Among his more well-known summations of this philosophy was the statement, "The goal is nothing, the movement is everything."

Among those within the socialist movement who challenged Bernstein was Rosa Luxemburg. In a classic work written in 1899, <u>Social Reform or Revolution</u>, she declared:

"It is absolutely false and totally unhistorical to represent work for reforms as a drawn-out revolution, and revolution as a condensed series of reforms. A social transformation and a legislative reform do not differ according to their <u>duration</u> but according to their <u>essence</u>. The whole secret of historical transformations through the utilization of political power consists precisely in the change of simple quantitative modification into a new quality, or to speak more concretely, in the transition from one historical period, one social order, to another.

"He who pronounces himself in favor of the method of legal reforms <u>in place of and as opposed to</u> the conquest of political power and social revolution does not really choose a more tranquil, surer and slower road to the <u>same</u> goal. He chooses a <u>different</u> goal. Instead of taking a stand for the establishment of a new social order, he takes a stand for surface modifications of the old order. . . not to the realization of the <u>socialist</u> order, but to the reform of <u>capitalism</u>; not to the suppression of the wage system, but to the diminution of exploitation; in a word, to the elimination of the abuses of capitalism instead of to that of capitalism itself." (1)

In the 100 years since these words were written, history has proven that capitalism cannot be reformed into a non-exploitative, non-oppressive system. Capitalism rules the world today, and look at the world! To the honest student of history and society, there can be little question about the need for a fundamentally <u>different</u> society, what usually goes by the name of socialism. Making "surface modifications" or "legislative reforms" without getting at the root of the problem—the ownership and control of the economy, as well as of the mass media, educational and cultural institutions and the government by the capitalist elite—is like spinning one's wheels in the sand.

Why have, and do, so many intelligent, well-meaning, dedicated activists and organizers continue down this dead-end road today?

The roots of this problem are deep. Ironically, part of these roots lie in the granting of the vote in 1787 to white, male workers in the United States. On the one hand this development gave these workers some influence over government, at least in the beginning decades of the U.S.A. But it also meant that the political alienation, and the political radicalism, of European working-class movements of the same time had no clear parallel in this country. This absence has had an historical effect that continues up to the present day.

Alexis De Tocqueville, writing in the 1830s, was surprisingly prescient about the effect of this reform. In <u>Democracy in America</u>, he "warned the American people of a basic inconsistency in their democratic way of life—an inconsistency which, unless speedily remedied, would probably result in the destruction of democracy. . . 'It is vain to summon a people, which has been rendered so dependent on the central power, to choose from time to time the representatives of that power; this rare and brief exercise of their free choice, however important it may be, will not prevent them from gradually losing the faculties of thinking, feeling, and acting for themselves, and thus gradually falling below the level of humanity.'" (2)

In addition, the reality of the North American continent as one with tremendous natural resources and great natural wealth meant that, as the indigenous Native American peoples were destroyed or displaced, there was a certain amount of "sharing" of that wealth throughout the European-American population that came to the New World. This "sharing" was certainly done in an uneven way; life for the vast majority of European-Americans, not to mention Africans, Latinos and Asian/Pacific Islanders, as well as Indigenous peoples, has been economically difficult for most of U.S. history. But it has been the case that the material wealth of this society has allowed the ruling elite to use some of that wealth to buy off and coopt serious challenges to their policies and their rule.

In the latter half of the 1940s and '50s many labor leaders and significant numbers of workers were "brought into line" through a combination of an anti-communist witchhunt—a full-scale assault by the government on almost everyone on the political Left—and cooptation through economic rewards from big business in exchange for labor peace and cooperation. A similar thing happened with the civil rights movement of the '50s and '60s, as seen by many former civil rights leaders who, today, are unabashed apologists for the system. Many of them were coopted through jobs they were given in the so-called "Great Society" anti-poverty programs of Lyndon Johnson. Others were appointed to well-paying jobs in various government agencies. I know from personal experience of a number of peace movement and student leaders from the 1960s who changed deeply-held political ideas in the '70s to conform to the changed political climate. From leaders of movements challenging a corrupt status quo they became committed Democrats unwilling to rock the boat while supportive of legislative reforms whose effect has been minimal.

Today, as we enter a new century, the same thing is going on. Cooptation, selling out, taking the easy way, self-delusion, and downright abandonment of socialist, revolutionary or even honestly progressive

-20-

ideas—this describes what is happening with a significant number of people who should know better.

To be fair, we need to acknowledge that it is not easy to be a full-time revolutionary; it is actually impossible for most people, in the sense of all one's work being organizing work for fundamental social change. People need to survive; they need to work within the economic system that exists. Although some jobs are less exploitative and more consistent with humanistic and socialist principles than others, it's a reality that work within exploitative institutions just to survive is a necessity for many people with consciously socialist ideas and ideals.

The problem occurs when people still have those ideas/ideals but fail to act on them, are unwilling to organize on their job against practices or structures that are clearly unjust or oppressive, or are willing to make compromises with those ideas/ideals so they can move up within the oppressive institutions for personal gain.

Many people who once had the socialist vision have lost it. They no longer believe that it will be possible to transform this society to any significant degree, and they have decided instead to do the best they can for themselves and their families, while also, in some cases, doing what can be done to support or be involved with progressive causes.

Others who never really identified themselves with the ideals of socialism, but who nevertheless are genuinely concerned about what they see around them and want to do something positive to change those conditions, join organizations that have much more limited goals. In part this is because of the absence of any visible socialist, or even a united progressive, movement or organization within their area and/or within the country.

This more limited approach has its material basis in the reality of advanced capitalist society. In the words of German socialist Hans Holz, "Limited goals such as those pursued by citizen initiatives, for example, seem more sensible than complex problems of complete social change. In this respect the level of consciousness has clearly changed from what it was since the great beginnings of the labor movement. The mode of production of late capitalism did not change anything in the dualistic structure of class antagonism (workers vs. capitalists), but it has spread over this structure the appearance of plurality and the illusion of individualization. Its character must be exposed again." (3)

Does this mean that it is wrong to work for reforms? Is it wrong to work to make it easier for workers to organize unions and go on strike without being fired? For women and people of color to have increased opportunities for employment and advancement on the job? For an end to discrimination against people with a different emotional/sexual orientation? For a universal, quality health care program available to all regardless of income? For decent housing, child care, safe communities, clean air and water?

Of course not. And not only because it is important to give specific content to the general objective of fundamental social change, for people to know specifically what it is we are working and fighting for. It is necessary to work for reforms because unless we can win victories, show people that it is possible by organization to achieve improvements, or at least defeat attempts to make our lives even worse, it is highly unlikely that they will be willing to join with us to achieve the much more difficult revolutionary objectives.

The key question is this: how do we work for reforms in a way which advances the movement for fundamental social change, towards a liberating society?

The answer to this question has three main components.

1) Work around issues and for reforms must build no illusions. In most instances, because of the dominance of big corporations over most institutions of society, it is not difficult to make a connection between the specific issue being addressed and the overall problem of an unjust system. In many cases it's not so much that activists need to "educate the masses" as much as it is that "the masses" need to see somebody willing to stand up with them against injustice and be vocal about the truth of the root of the problem.

As much as possible there should be a process of education and consciousness-raising that goes with the work around issues. Of course, there are limitations on the extent to which consciousness-raising can be done by a particular organization at particular times, e.g., if a group needs to tone down its language because of a tactical decision that around a particular struggle this is the correct approach to take. But this muted approach cannot become the modus operandi of the group in general. If it does, it opens the door to opportunistic and unprincipled behavior which, in the long run, will undercut the original good intentions with which the group was formed.

2) We need to build organizations, whether it be trade unions, commu-

nity organizations, or single-issue and constituency-based organizations, that are <u>fiercely independent</u> and <u>broadly democratic</u>. You can't have one without the other. Together they can keep the group and individuals within the group from falling prey to the seductive, cooptive lures of the system, keep everyone focused on the prize of a genuinely democratic, people-oriented society.

Democracy means much more than just periodic elections for leadership. Elections are important, but in the absence of conscious efforts and mechanisms to inform those voting and encourage active participation in between elections, they are little more than a hollow shell.

Democracy means the encouragement of discussion on a broad scale about key issues, including the articulation and circulation of differing positions. If it is only the views of the current leadership which are being circulated, and differences within the leadership group are withheld from the broader membership, this will inevitably lead to paternalistic or hierarchical, undemocratic forms of organization.

It is important that there be flexible but firm time limits on people speaking in meetings to discourage the monopolization of discussion by articulate, long-winded individuals. This is not a small issue. If time is not consciously provided for all those who wish to speak and limited for those who tend to go on and on, those not used to speaking will feel intimidated and discouraged from active involvement.

The employment of a small-group discussion format, when possible, helps to make it easier for those afraid or not used to speaking up in large groups to find their voice. This is a way of including those who can easily feel excluded. Sometimes the best format is a mix of small-group and large-group discussions, with report-backs from the small groups to the large group.

Wherever possible, a consensus-seeking method of discussion should be used. This discourages "show-boating" between individuals trying to get across their individual point and encourages a more collective process of listening and healthy interaction.

Finally, collective evaluation is an essential part of a genuinely democratic process. In this way those who are making mistakes or errors can have them corrected, and a process is established in which everyone comes to understand that no one individual is above the group.

3) If both of these aspects are working effectively, then the third aspect

will follow: the <u>development and training of new leadership</u> within the organization. Organizations which are not able to bring new people forward, especially young people, are organizations that are not going to survive as independent, democratic and educational institutions. It is true that power corrupts. Those who remain in positions of leadership too long, with few exceptions, tend to lose touch with what might have been the best of intentions, and with those they claim to be speaking and working for.

It is not easy to build these kinds of organizations. The relatively low level of socialist—or even independent progressive—consciousness within the society often translates into problems as far as the way in which progressive, grass-roots, labor or even socialist organizations function. Many organizations which say they are about challenging the status quo, or standing up for the rights of workers, low-income people, people of color, women, lesbians/gays, etc. tend to have a schizophrenic character.

On the one hand, they can be strong, hard-working, even militant at times, in struggling for the particular demands, needs and policy changes that would benefit those they represent. Individual members and leaders of the organizing group can make tremendous sacrifices, going above and beyond the call of duty, in an effort to bring about change.

And yet, when it comes to relating to elected officials, or supporting people trying to be elected officials, and when it comes to the <u>internal</u> relationships among those within the group, the methods of operation can be very similar to those of the system which is the source of the problems and crises they are struggling to change in the first place.

What are some of those "methods of operation?"

Despite lip service to democracy as the preferred method of operation, real power within the organization can reside in the hands of one individual or a small group. There is no genuine effort to involve others in the process of decision-making, to train others to learn how to give leadership, or to give others opportunities for on-the-job training in leadership skills once they have developed to a point where they are ready to give leadership.

Elected officials, or those running for office, are accorded "first among equals" status by the organization's leadership even if they are inconsistent in the ways in which they interact with and respect the people and the organizations which provide the votes to get them into office. There is little accountability because there is little demanded. The relationship is a hierarchical relationship similar to the capitalist/patriarchal/racist model.

Information and inputs which are necessary in order to make informed decisions are not shared with the membership, or even the broader leadership, by the core leadership, leading to a concentration of power and, eventually, alienation on the part of that membership even if they agree with the stated purposes of the organization.

The internal dynamics of the organization are much more competitive than cooperative. Individuals use their intelligence, their facility with words, their charisma, their access to funding sources, their greater experience not to help the group as a whole grow as a whole but to advance their personal agendas or careers. People who disagree with leadership views or decisions, who honestly try to state their point of view on a relevant matter, are subject to put-downs, humiliation, being ignored or, in the worst case, personal abuse.

These destructive forms of leadership are often, although not always, to be found coming from men, particularly white men, and even more particularly white non-working-class men. Those who have been raised to believe that they are "better" than those "under" them, or who have been raised in circumstances of greater privilege, are naturally going to believe that they should give leadership, and they are also logically going to go about it in the same kinds of ways that they have been trained.

This style of leadership must be actively combatted. It is a fundamental obstacle to the changes needed.

There is a crucial need for what Italian revolutionary Antonio Gramsci called, "a new set of standards, a new psychology, new ways of feeling, thinking and living that must be specific to the working class. . . a new culture, that is, for a new moral life that cannot but be intimately connected to a new intuition of life, until it becomes a new way of feeling and seeing reality." (4)

There are elements in traditional working-class culture, including and very importantly the cultures of African Americans and other communities of color, which can be drawn upon in the construction of this "new culture," in the making of what can only be called a cultural revolution within the progressive movement, so essential to combating reformism and moving toward fundamental social transformation.

Traditional working-class culture* is centered around people, not things. It holds up love between two people (almost always a man and a woman), a close and loving family, sincere friendships, relationships with the natural world as the most important things in life. This is distinct from the dominant culture of capitalism which holds up the accumulation of more and more things, products and objects as the goal in life.

This is not to romanticize working-class culture. There is also sexism, racism, homophobia and other forms of backwards thinking within it. But underneath those negative things there are the positive elements that can be appealed to and which provide hope that the negatives can be confronted and changed. This has certainly been true for many working-class people over the past few decades as the civil rights/Black liberation movement, the women's movement, the gay/lesbian rights movement and other social movements challenged old patterns of thinking and acting.

The positive aspects of this culture have been undercut by the tentacles of the corporate monster which reach into so many areas of life, with television playing a major role in that process. The cultural values of the rich are being taken up by too many working-class people. In the words of Charley Young, a working class community organizer in Dallas, Texas:

"We are taught to be highly individualistic, to the point of helping ourselves before or at the expense of others, and the rights of individuals are placed above the rights of the society.

"We should be proud of our culture and our heritage. It is the working people who have done the work and who are doing the work to give this country the potential it has. And now, especially as the time of the Second American Revolution approaches, we must set about to do the work which will lay a basis for a more democratic and a more people-oriented system. To do this we must have a positive and creative understanding of our culture, and we must pitch in and set about to help build a progressive, secure future for those we are proud to love: our families, our friends, our people. We must not abandon our cultural values." (5)

---

*When the phrase, "working-class culture" is used here, it is important to underline that we are referring to both the cultures of communities of color, which are overwhelmingly composed of working-class people, and distinct white working-class cultures.

Working-class people, or those from middle- or upper-class backgrounds who are willing to genuinely open themselves to constructive criticism, willing to learn from and respect the leadership of working-class people, especially women and people of color, must be encouraged to give leadership to this movement for a Second American Revolution. But this alone won't bring about the new culture which Gramsci wrote about. There must be a conscious effort made to connect up with the positive working-class traditions Charley Young talks about, as well as building upon the important insights about process, new ways of work, new relationships, coming out of the women's movement of the recent past and present. Communities of color in the United States are also rich in cultural traditions of great value in the construction of this new culture crossing lines of race, gender, class and sexual orientation. Together, connecting and interconnecting, inspiring and motivating, these old traditions and the new alliance culture which can take shape within a popular alliance as it grows and develops, are bedrock necessities to counter the dangers of reformism that have historically sidetracked many efforts to bring about positive social change.

But the development of this new culture is not enough. We need to bring together millions of people into an organized, popular critical mass prepared to work together politically to bring about change. Where are these millions going to come from?

Footnotes

1) Rosa Luxemburg, "Social Reform or Revolution," Selected Political Writings, edited by Dick Howard, Monthly Review Press, pps. 115-116

2) Quoted in Saul Alinsky, Reveille for Radicals, Vintage Books, pps. 44-45

3) Hans Heinz Holz, "The Downfall and Future of Socialism," Nature, Society and Thought, Vol. 5, No. 3, pps. 54-55

4) Antonio Gramsci, Selections from Cultural Writings, Harvard University Press, pps. 41 and 98

5) Charley Young, "The Coming of the 2nd American Revolution," quoted in the Green Mountain Quarterly, No. 5, February, 1977, p. 69

A POPULAR ALLIANCE AS THE WAY FORWARD

The development of an independent, popular alliance is the essence of a winning strategy for the United States. What else could have a chance of victory? The ruling elite in the U.S. has tremendous financial resources, a huge intelligence and military apparatus, and it controls the mass media and many educational institutions. To overcome such a powerful enemy, it will take the united and unified strength of millions, if not tens of millions of people.

Who are the sectors of the population that would make up such an alliance, such a popular critical mass?

Clearly, significant sectors of the U.S. working class must be part of a popular alliance for change. As the largest group of people in the country, upwards of 75% or so of the population, and as a group which is forced to sell its "labor power" in order to survive, there is a very concrete interest in a new society genuinely set up to uphold "life, liberty and the pursuit of happiness" rather than profit, individualistic gain and abuse of others for private enrichment.

Yet it would be a mistake, for many reasons, to take the <u>objective</u> reality of the working class as the largest social force with an interest in change and make that into a rigid strategic commitment to the working class <u>as a whole</u> as the leading element of the social change movement.

The first, most obvious reason, is that within this large social force are found a wide disparity of ideas and ideologies as to what is wrong with this country and what needs to be done to change it. Many white, male workers look upon people of color and women as basically rivals, competitors for their jobs, their incomes, or their neighborhoods. Racism, sexism and homophobia are widespread among this white, male sector of the overall working class, even if there has been some positive change in recent years within this group. This sector, generally, tends to be supportive of an aggressive, militaristic foreign policy, although there is much less willingness than in previous years to sacrifice the lives of their children in long, drawn-out wars. Basic principles of unionism, "an injury to one is an injury to all," do not have deep roots among this sector, as witness the abysmally low rate—about 10%—of union membership among privately-employed workers.

Historically, for most of the 20th century, it has <u>not</u> been the labor movement which has been in the vanguard of struggles for social change.

The exceptions to this rule were the Industrial Workers of the World (the Wobblies) in the period prior to World War I and the period of the 1930s and 1940s when the Congress of Industrial Organizations (CIO) achieved tremendous strides in union organization and political strength. Without the CIO Franklin D. Roosevelt could not have been re-elected three times and the progressive social reforms enacted into law that, despite recent, and continuing, weakening, still remain. However, with the conscious implementation by the administrations of Harry Truman (Democratic) and Dwight Eisenhower (Republican) of domestic and international, anti-Communist, Cold War policies after World War II, most of the Left-led CIO unions were destroyed. By the mid-'50s, with the CIO merger into the AFL-CIO, the labor movement was politically tamed.

It was around this same period of time, in the mid-1950s, that large numbers of African American working people in the South began to demand their human and civil rights under the leadership of Martin Luther King, Jr. and others. In 1955 the Montgomery, Alabama bus boycott electrified the country and led to the emergence of a mass movement based in the African American working class. Although in the first years of its emergence this movement, for the most part, was led by non-working-class people,* especially ministers and students, there is no question about the class composition of the movement itself. Over time, as it moved into the North in particular, indigenous working-class leaders emerged, and some long-time black unionists played important roles all the way throughout, from its earliest beginnings.

Throughout U.S. American history the African American community has been a major force in resisting the worst of U.S. capitalist exploitation—since they are on the receiving end of "the worst"—and pushing the entire country in a more progressive direction. It is an historical fact that this social force, the African American community, because of its role and place within the economy, its reality as an overwhelmingly working-class community, its traditions of resistance, and its less individu-

---

*One major exception is E.D. Nixon. Nixon was an older trade union and civil rights leader living and working in Montgomery, Alabama at the time Rosa Parks refused to move from her seat on the bus. Those who were there credit Nixon with key organizational leadership, including the recruitment and building of support for Dr. Martin Luther King, Jr. to become the leading spokesperson for what was to become the Montgomery movement.

alistic and more communal culture has been a catalytic and essential force in the struggle for positive change.

Antonio Gramsci, the brilliant Italian revolutionary, wrote about the need to go beyond a stale and static approach toward the working class when developing revolutionary strategy. In the words of Carl Boggs, "In political terms, Gramsci was convinced that the transition to socialism would be something other than a 'pure' form of class struggle between wage-labor and capital; more likely, it would be a complex mediated process involving a dynamic constellation of interests and goals perhaps having little pre-defined relationship to specific class structures. He rejected as metaphysics the assumption that particular classes are the necessary historical bearers of a revolutionary consciousness, or that such attributes could be ascertained in advance, on the basis of a universal logic." (1)

The consistent, catalytic and leading role of the African American community in U.S. history bears witness to Gramsci's perspectives. Agitation and direct action against slavery in the first half of the 19th century led to the Civil War and the legal end of chattel slavery. Reconstruction governments in the South after the Civil War, in which newly-elected blacks led successful efforts to enact reforms that benefited not just newly-freed slaves but poor whites as well, were the precursor to the mass, multi-racial populist movement of the late 1800s. The black nationalist Marcus Garvey movement of the 1920s almost certainly impacted upon the multi-racial CIO labor movement of the '30s. The civil rights movement of the '50s and '60s had direct and indirect connections to the emergence of the women's movement, the student movement and the anti-Vietnam War movements, as well as the Chicano, Puerto Rican, American Indian, Asian/Pacific Islander, lesbian/gay/bisexual/transgender rights and other mass movements of the '60s and '70s. And finally, the black-led Rainbow Coalition movement of the '80s helped to generate the political energy for the development of the major national third party groups of the '90s, the Green Party, the Labor Party, the New Party and the Campaign for a New Tomorrow.

What are other key sectors of this popular alliance?

Clearly other communities of color—Native Americans, the Puerto Rican, Chicano/Mexican and other Latino communities, Asian/Pacific Islanders—have similarities to the African American community. A large majority of the members of these communities are working-class people, many of them low-income. The reality of structural racism has led to their

-30-

second-class treatment and, as a result, more of a readiness in comparison to European Americans to organize against injustice and unequal treatment. They maintain distinct cultures which serve as a source of support and which transmit values that often go against the grain of me-first capitalism.

This is not to lump all cultures of people of color into one big, amalgamated, "other" culture as if they were cut out of the same cloth. At the same time that there are many similarities in relation to the dominant white bourgeois culture, there are also distinctions. There are tensions and conflicts between people from these different communities, just as there are between whites and non-whites.

It is also the case that there are class differences within these communities. Although there are virtually no people of color who belong to the dominant corporate elite, the top 1/2 of 1% (or less) of the population, there are a small number of people of color who have made it big economically and a larger group, if still a significant minority, who are upper-middle-class in income and occupation.

However, the reality of endemic, deep-seated racism within the U.S. economic, social and political system has meant that these different social/cultural groups often function as distinct groups, not as workers, or some other economic class category. Because of their reality as predominantly working-class communities, combined with their experience with institutionalized racism, their political perspective tends to be progressive on most, if not all, issues. These are clearly essential components of a potentially vibrant popular alliance.

Women, over half of the population, are the other major social force which is an indispensable part of the alliance needed so desperately.

Many women today are also workers. More than one half of the population in communities of color are women. Yet for at least 150 years in the United States, for as long as there has been one form or another of socialist organization, there have been women's rights organizations dedicated to the achievement of women's equality. Women have long seen the need for their own forms of organization to advance their demands.

Entrenched sexism, with roots reaching back historically much deeper than racism, is the motivation for organized women's efforts toward equality. The forms that sexism take are many, from wife-beating and rape, to economic discrimination and verbal harassment, to legal discrimination and psychological abuse. Organizations and movements have existed and continue to exist to deal with these problems.

Conversely, within many, if not most, of the great social change movements in this country women have played major roles, whether it be the labor movement of the 1930s (often as so-called "women's auxiliaries"), the civil rights movement of the '50s and '60s, or the student and anti-war movements of the '60s and '70s. They have functioned both autonomously and together to advance a progressive agenda.

In addition to the basic nuts-and-bolts work, the speaking, writing and organizing, women bring to a larger progressive movement crucial insights about process, about ways of working together in a cooperative way, about connecting stated objectives and a way of working and relating to one another which lives up to those objectives. During the late 1960s the women's movement came forward with the simple yet profound observation, and with the demand that, "the personal is political." Men who say they are about a different, egalitarian and loving society need to act that way now, or it's all a sham. These are insights without which we have no hope, absolutely none, of building a permanent alliance capable of contesting for power and transforming this society.

There are other sectors which make up the prospective alliance. Each brings particular insights and experiences, special energies, wisdom or knowledge.

Farmers are a very small percentage of the population, no more than 2%, but in the '70s and '80s they were a visible, militant force resisting the wholesale displacement of small and even medium-size farmers from their land by banks and government financial institutions. In many localities they built alliances with local labor unions and urban-based community organizations.

Within traditional Marxism farmers and rural people have tended to be looked upon with suspicion. They are too religious; the conditions of their lives tend to make them individualistic and "petty-bourgeois," to use the vernacular. Yet within countries that have had revolutions and tried to build socialism, solving the so-called "peasant question" has been crucial to the success, or lack of success, of the efforts at social transformation.

The bottom-line fact is that it is extremely difficult to own a farm these days and make a go of it without working 70-80 hours a week. Even then many do not make it. It is not an easy life. Farmers, and former farmers who want to return to the land, are as much in need of social and economic transformation as workers, women, and people of color.

Youth, young people who are coming up through school, do not have much of a future to look forward to in this world of global warming and massive injustice. Statistics indicate that many youth who graduate from college or even graduate school need to continue living with their parents for years because they cannot afford the cost of a new home if they can find a steady job. This has been true for many young people even during the supposed "good times" of the 1990s.

Violence and youth-on-youth crime is a major problem, particularly in low-income/working-class communities. AIDS and the HIV virus threaten their sexual identities and their very lives, at the same time that movies, TV shows, videos, periodicals and music blare out sexual, sexist messages encouraging them to "act adult" by screwing around.

But young people are not accepting the script that is being handed to them by the powers-that-be. Around many different issues—Central American and South African solidarity, women's rights, anti-racism, environmental issues, lesbian/gay/sexual minority issues, immigrant rights, sweatshops and the unjust global capitalist economy—young people have been active. Young people bring to the progressive movement new perspectives and new energy that are valuable for us all. They are an essential component of a winning alliance.

Seniors are numerically one of the largest groups within U.S. society, and many of them have a difficult time of it. This is not just because of the natural process of deterioration of the body and mind which all of us, sooner or later, experience. It is also because many suffer from a system which uses their labor in their younger years and then forces them to live on very low incomes once they are no longer useful to employers. Furthermore, there are limited numbers of programs available to help them deal with the daily problems of their lives, and what programs do exist are having funds cut by local, state and federal governments.

The United States is a wealthy country and there is no excuse for the difficulties older people are forced to endure. We need a society which treasures seniors as people with wisdom to pass on to younger generations and deserving of concrete forms of respect and appreciation to make their later years meaningful and dignified.

The gay/lesbian/bi/trans movement is one of the most recent of the new social movements to emerge over the past 40 years, although semi-underground gay and lesbian groups go back much further. It is a movement that experiences overt and violent repression both from individual, homophobic men, and from organized, reactionary, right-wing groups, as well as institutionalized and government discrimination.

This movement calls into question some of the most basic cultural assumptions of the dominant culture. It demands that heterosexual people open their minds and their emotions to a reality lived by those who have different emotional/sexual orientations. It demands tolerance, at the least, and a basic respect for the rights and lives of those who are different that is difficult for many U.S. Americans to deal with.

The social transformation and the new society we are working to create is about nothing if it is not about new, loving and caring, human relationships with one another, replacing approaches of competition and attempted dominance with cooperation and equality. The gay/lesbian/bi/trans movement has a natural and vital place within the popular alliance.

People with disabilities have developed a broad-based, cross-race and cross-class movement in recent years. Upwards of 50 million people in the United States have some kind of disability, and every day, unfortunately, more people lose limbs or are injured on the job or in some other way.

People with disabilities challenge basic assumptions of the dominant culture which holds up handsome, attractive, "together" women and men as examples of success. If someone has a disability, how can they ever climb the corporate ladder, or become a successful role model?

But as people with disabilities have pointed out, one can have a beautiful face and a great body but have a heart like a stone. Sometimes the disabilities that are the most damaging, to other people and to oneself, ultimately, are ones that cannot be seen.

All people should have the right to live a decent life and develop their talents to the best of their abilities. This is what the movement of people with disabilities is working for. These are demands that are sound and winnable, after the relationships of power have been overturned and a process of social transformation has been initiated. The movement working for them deserves support and respect now as they struggle for their rights.

Finally, the environmental movement is a crucial movement today. Tremendous damage is being done to our home, the earth. Large businesses and transnational corporations have seriously polluted the land, water and air.

The "greenhouse effect," caused by a geometrical increase in carbon dioxide and industrial pollutants over recent decades, could warm up the earth several degrees over the next 50 years, leading to a partial melting of the polar ice caps, a rise of the oceans, major social and economic dislocation and massive famine as crop-growing regions become prone to regular droughts.

The ozone hole over Antarctica, also caused by the transnational-dominated industrial economy, is continuing to grow, reaching into parts of South America, jeopardizing millions of people with ultraviolet rays from the sun and a major escalation of cancer rates.

Nuclear power and nuclear weapons production plants continue to operate, threatening another Three Mile Island, Chernobyl or worse. Many animal and plant species are threatened with extinction. Our natural environment is facing a steady deterioration towards a potentially apocalyptic series of catastrophes.

In response to this urgent reality, as well as to locality-specific problems of toxic land, water and air, a powerful movement has emerged to protect our health and the earth's viability. In recent years it has become more and more a movement based in working-class and people-of-color communities as the massiveness of the problem of hazardous waste that comes with advanced industrial capitalist society leads to massive health problems in communities all over the country.

This is a movement which is different than the others listed above in that it is "issue-oriented" as distinct from the others which are more movements of particular social groupings or sectors of the population. It crosses all the lines of class, race, gender, age, disability, sexual orientation, occupation, etc. because we are all threatened by what is being done to our environment. It is a fundamental issue needing our urgent attention.

We are still left with a number of questions, however. One of the major ones is how the bringing together of this alliance of different, although overlapping, sectors of the population relates to more traditional Marxist notions of class struggle between the capitalists and the workers. More to the point, what is the working class today, and what are the potentialities for its different sectors to see the importance of this popular alliance?

Footnote

1) Carl Boggs, The Two Revolutions: Gramsci and the Dilemmas of Western Marxism, South End Press, p. 229

CLASS STRUCTURE
AND A POPULAR ALLIANCE

Many of these various component parts of the potential popular alliance are made up primarily of working-class people. Much of the traditional Left sees its primary task as being the uniting of the working class. It would be helpful, in trying to get a better handle on how this alliance concept relates to that more traditional concept, to look more closely at the working class in the U.S. today and the U.S. class structure. In this way we can have a better sense of the interrelationships among class, culture, gender and other distinctions and divisions between people who, long-term, have a common interest in revolutionary change.

Karl Marx was among the first to identify the working class as a key sector, particularly the industrial working class which was growing in numbers in the mid-1800s as the industrial revolution advanced in Europe and elsewhere. Marx saw this sector of the population as <u>the</u> key revolutionary sector for several reasons.

First, industry was concentrating large numbers of people, by the hundreds and thousands, into factories where the workers shared the common experience of exploitation of their labor by the owners of the factories. Because of this shared common exploitation, over time the industrial working class, and other workers influenced by them even if not in as stark or clear-cut a situation as workers in large factories, would come to see the power in their hands due to their crucial role in the functioning of capitalist society. In Marx's line of reasoning, and that of many revolutionaries who came after him, this situation was distinct from the realities of life for peasants, farmers, artisans and craftspeople who may have been poor, but whose conditions of life did not teach them the lesson of <u>collective organization</u> as the means toward improving those conditions.

Connected to this was the visible reality of the extraction of "surplus value" from the collective group of factory workers, and other workers, by the dominant capitalists. "Surplus value" refers to the labor time put in by workers above and beyond what is needed in order to pay for their subsistence. If, for example, it took four hours of labor time for a worker to be paid wages sufficient to keep himself (and his family) alive*, and the

---

*In the time in which Marx was writing the workers he was talking about were, overwhelmingly, men.

worker worked eight hours, those additional four hours of labor accrued to the benefit of the factory owner in the form of products produced that he is able to sell and make a profit on above and beyond the products sold to pay the four hours to keep the worker alive. This is the surplus value to the capitalist.

Marx saw this industrial working class growing to the point where there would be a vast gulf between the great majority of exploited workers and the tiny minority of private property-owning capitalists. In other words, over time the working class would become and would learn that it was the dominant class in terms of numbers. This, combined with the experience of working together in the factories and learning how to struggle together against the capitalists for improvements in their lives, were the major reasons for the Marxist determination that the unification and enlightenment, through experience and training, of the working class, particularly the industrial working class, was the way in which capitalism would be replaced by socialism.

On the face of it, there are transparent difficulties with a couple of the key components of this theoretical/ strategic perspective when it comes to United States realities today. First, the number of workers in factories has been going down as automation, robots and computerization increasingly take over industrial processes within many industries. Second, the "industrial proletariat" is hardly the dominant group numerically <u>even within the overall working class</u>, much less the population as a whole. Government workers, retail salespeople, office employees, health sector workers, truck drivers, those in so-called "service" industries—these are much more the types of jobs that are growing in numbers and are projected to continue to do so for years to come.

The U.S. working class, however, those who own no significant income-generating property and must work for others for a living, is a <u>decided</u> majority, taking all of the many occupations and sectors into account. Estimates by economists who have studied this question put its total range between 70-80% of the adult working population. It excludes less than 10% who are self-employed, as well as "officials and the managers perhaps down to the level of foremen, in order to remove from the working class the controllers and organizers of the enterprises and their managerial agents." (1) It includes:

- construction workers of many different job categories
- workers in basic industry: steel, electrical, rubber, car, truck, and bus production, textiles, etc.

- workers in hospitals, health clinics and other medical and dental care occupations
- salespeople, retail clerks and cashiers
- elementary, junior high and high school teachers, and some teachers in colleges and universities
- farmworkers and workers in the food production and distribution industry
- office workers of many different skill levels and occupations
- computer data entry and programming personnel
- waitresses and waiters, janitors, dishwashers, motel and hotel workers
- carpenters, machinists, ironworkers, toolmakers, weavers and tailors
- workers in local, state and federal government, in scores of different agencies, divisions and types of work
- drivers of trucks, taxis, limousines, subway trains, railroads, buses, planes, and trolley cars
- miners of coal, uranium, and other minerals and metals, loggers and lumbermen(people)
- telephone operators, repairpeople, sales people and telemarketers
- workers in banking, insurance, financial investments, real estate, advertising and other marketing industries
- employees in television, radio, newspaper, magazine and book publishing, movie production and distribution, and other components of the communications industry

Within this huge group are found many differences and divisions, as we have touched on above. These differences have been used by the ruling corporate elite historically and today to keep this working class, this class that <u>does</u> have a common interest in a different kind of society, from uniting <u>as a class</u> in a joint struggle for positive, people-oriented, fundamental social change.

The fact is that the level of <u>class consciousness</u>, an understanding of the common interests of working-class people and the nature of and way in which the class system functions, is very low in the United States, generally speaking. There are certainly <u>some</u> commonalities in perspective. There is widespread anger at government and big business, although it is balanced by a continuing, if declining, belief by many workers that if they just work harder or get a lucky break, like winning the lottery, they, individually, will be able to rise out of their condition. Workers in particular workplaces generally understand that it's an "us vs. them" situation when it comes to the bosses in their particular workplace, but that does not always, or even often, translate into making connections with other workers in different workplaces.

There is such a thing as working-class culture, or to be more accurate, working class cultures because of the various nationalities and races that make up the U.S. working class, but some of the more positive aspects of those cultures—straightforwardness, concern for others of at least one's family or primary group, emotional honesty—have been affected by the dominance of the often brutal, sexist, racist, and individualistic mass culture propagated by those who own the cultural institutions and mass communications industries.

In addition, there can be no denying that there has been some, if not a lot of, "social mobility" within U.S. society, particularly for white males and, over the past 25 or so years, some women and people of color. Yet the social mobility is within very definite limits. How many people born in public housing projects have ever joined the boards of major transnational corporations? Those who have done so are infinitesimal in numbers. And the decided, long-term trend in the U.S. economy today is not up but down for most people. Growing numbers have experienced declining incomes and a fall out of the middle class because of the changes taking place within the economy.

What are the basic socio-economic classes in U.S. society? If we can give a reasonably accurate answer to this question, we will be in a much better position to understand who has the most class interest in revolutionary change, who is somewhere in the middle, and who is definitely on the other side of the class divide.

Classes in U.S. Society

In my view, there are seven basic class groupings in U.S. society.

1) **The barely-surviving working class:** These are the people, a large majority of them people of color due to institutionalized racism, who rarely can secure jobs for any significant period of time. For some their "work," their means of livelihood, is crime or street hustling, often drug-connected. Some are homeless. Some drop out or are forced out of school while in their teens because of pregnancy, a personal or family trauma, peer pressure, indifferent schools, etc. Some are prostitutes, some are on welfare. Some have emotional, mental or physical disabilities that have not been treated or even diagnosed. Many have been in prison or go in and out. Some are able to find odd jobs from time to time but have a

difficult time making ends meet because of the minimal pay they receive and poor working conditions, so that their jobs tend not to last very long.

This is a group whose lives have become more difficult over the past 15-20 years as right-wing government policies have undercut or destroyed many of the social programs that were having some impact on helping certain individuals rise out of this class. These policies have also led to a massive explosion in the number of people in prison, now up to 2 million from just 600,000 at the beginning of the '80s.

This group has a definite, compelling interest in revolutionary change. Historically it has provided some of the leadership and membership of resistance movements, e.g., Malcolm X, the Black Panther Party, the Young Lords and welfare rights organizations of the '60s and '70s.

Because of the economic difficulties and insecurity of their lives, as well as because in most cases they are not joined together on a day-to-day basis with other people in a workplace, this is a group which can "come and go" into and out of progressive political activity more rapidly than workers with relatively secure employment and housing. Yet it is a sector of the working class that must be present in significant numbers within the popular alliance if only because they have a gut-level understanding of the need for fundamental, systemic change, and because they have the most to gain from a popular revolution; if their lives do not change after a "revolution," there hasn't been one.

2) **The low-income working class:** This is a very large group, probably the largest grouping of the working class. It has been growing in recent years as huge layoffs within basic industry and among major corporations have become the rule, as production jobs are either moved overseas or are replaced by machines. The workers who used to receive high, working-class salaries and good benefits in these occupations—steel, auto, electronics, etc.—are often now working at jobs paying a great deal less. Most of the new jobs that are being created by the U.S. capitalist economy—upwards of 60% of them—are in this growing category. Many of them are part-time, temporary or on a contract basis, with no benefits.

Low-income generally means those workers who make, as a family, no more than $25,000-28,000 a year (for a family of four). With this amount of money it is very difficult to sustain a family of more than 3-4 people. It is almost impossible to put money away toward the childrens' college education. If there is no health insurance, or one which demands large co-payments or deductibles, a serious medical condition can wreak major havoc. A loss of job, or eviction from a house or apartment because of fire, loss of income, or illegal landlord action, can become a long-term personal or family disaster.

Some of the major types of jobs falling within this category include: some production workers, hospital and health care workers, retail clerks, salespeople and cashiers, office workers, computer entry workers, farmworkers, waitresses, cleaning people, janitors, lower-level government employees, many transportation workers, telephone operators, many workers in finance, real estate and advertising, lower-level workers within the telecommunications industry, receptionists and secretaries, some cultural workers.

Some of these occupations have a long history of unionization— production workers, health care, transportation, service employees, telecommunications, and government employees among them. Many of the workers within this sector are women and people of color, which generally means that they are more open to progressive political views. It was from this sector of the working class that much of the mass base came for movements like the civil rights movement coming out of the South in the '50s and '60s, or the Rainbow Coalition movement in the mid-'80s. This is clearly a key sector of the working class.

3) **The moderate-to-middle-income working class:** Since the merger of the AFL and the CIO in the 1950s it has been from this sector of the working class that the predominant leadership within the trade union movement has come. This sector tends to be more white and more male than the barely-surviving and low-income sectors of the working class, and therefore more middle-of-the-road and sometimes conservative politically. It was from this sector that many of the "Reagan Democrats" came.

Some of the job categories within this sector are: construction workers (particularly the skilled trades areas), some of those who have been working for a long time within basic industry, teachers in grades K-12 and some teachers in colleges and universities, computer programmers and analysts, other high-tech "knowledge" workers, some airlines employees, some workers within banking, insurance, real estate, advertising and finance, some communications industry employees.

Yet there is certainly a level of class consciousness within this grouping, if colored by forms of racism, sexism, homophobia and generally less progressive politics compared to other sectors. It is from within some of the job categeories within this sector that large numbers of people have been thrown out of work over the past 20-25 years as basic industry has downsized and/or moved jobs overseas. These are the people who have seen the cumulative tax load go up, while taxes on those above them making six-figure or higher salaries have been going down. Unfortunately, a sizeable number of this sector aim their anger at those below them, particularly those who are barely surviving or are recent immigrants to the U.S. This group has let racism, in particular, get in the way of unity against the common class enemy, the corporate/financial rulers.

"Moderate-to-middle-income" means in the range of the high twenties up to $50,000-$60,000 or higher. Those on the higher end of the scale tend to be more conservative, generally speaking, for understandable reasons.

This is a sector of the working class that is increasingly insecure about its future, due to the downsizing phenomenon referred to above, recent trade agreements like NAFTA and GATT, and the generally negative long-term trend of the economy and society. They can play an important role in a popular alliance, but more than with any other sector of the working class, many workers in this sector are in need of serious educational work around racism, sexism, homophobia and other destructive and divisive, ingrained ideologies.

4) **The property-owning, small/medium business class:** This sector includes farmers who have been able to stay on their land and make a go of it. It includes people who own businesses that are either family-run or have a relatively small number of employees in comparison to the giant corporations. It includes people who own a small number of properties which they rent out either part-time or full-time as money-making enterprises.

In general with this grouping, the degree of openness to progressive politics has to do with size, with the smaller farms and businesses tending to be more willing to work with community groups, unions, or progressive organizations of some kind; or, it has to do with gender, culture, and/or other non-class considerations. For example, African American businesspeople, even at a "medium" level of business success, are often willing to support movements and organizations that are dealing with the issues of the barely surviving or low-income workers. Women, speaking generally, due to their experiences of oppression, are more likely to sympathize with those who are not doing as well as they, as indicated by the "gender gap" when it comes to support of progressive initiatives.

In economic terms, this group does not have an easy time of it in the big business-dominated economy of the U.S.A. today. There is a lot of turnover among the lower-income levels of this sector; most new businesses have failed within two years of starting up. Reagan/Bush/Clinton economics have not been friendly to this sector, either; the prime beneficiaries of their policies have been the big business sector. Government regulations and bureaucracy can impose additional economic burdens on this sector, which can turn them off to the positive social objectives of regulation, e.g., environmental clean-up.

As with the middle-income sector of the working class, or at least the majority of this sector who are white and male, conservative ideology is relatively strong. This is not surprising. After all, these are people who have bought into the capitalist system and are trying to become successful capitalists, on a small scale, themselves. But this does not mean they should be written off by those working to effect fundamental social transformation. It is a fact that in most communities small businesspeople have political influence beyond their numbers. Their opinions carry weight. It is necessary to work with them and address their problems honestly. At the same time it is important that this sector not be the one calling the shots when it comes to strategy and tactics for change. Their investment in the system and its ideology means that they have more to lose than workers, and this affects their willingness to struggle in the ways which are sometimes necessary.

5) **The professional and managerial middle class:** This class includes doctors, dentists, lawyers, college and university teachers and administrators; middle, managerial levels of industrial, governmental, financial and corporate institutions; some of the "knowledge workers" in the computer, microelectronics and telecommunications industries; ministers; some artists, musicians, dancers and singers; non-governmental social service managers; and some elected officials and their employees. It is not a large class, percentage-wise, in comparison with the working class, but it is made up of people who, as with the property-owning middle class, have a lot of influence within communities. This is done through participation in voluntary organizations and local government bodies disproportionate to their numbers within the population as a whole, as well as through their more-likely participation within the political/electoral process.

This class, as a class, is not a potentially revolutionary class. Its members do too well economically within the capitalist system to be willing to rock the boat to the point where those material advantages might be threatened.

However, there are a significant number, if a minority, of the members of this class who are progressive, who are concerned about "the little guy," social and racial injustice, militarism, environmental degradation, etc. As with the property-owning middle-class this tends to be more true for women and people of color than for white men. These progressive middle-class people can play important roles in terms of financial support, active participation and/or individual leadership to progressive causes and even, in a much smaller number of cases, revolutionary groups.

That small percentage of this class which aligns with the revolutionary movement <u>can</u> play important, even crucial, roles within that movement, but there is a need for these individuals and the movement as a whole to recognize that their class position can lead to serious problems. People from non-working-class backgrounds need to understand how those backgrounds, or present-day experiences, ingrain negative traits such as elitism, hierarchical approaches to organization, racism and sexism (sometimes of a subtle but still negative character), competitiveness and paternalism. Time and time again over many years of effort to build a strong working-class movement in the U.S., these system-generated, elitist personal characteristics have derailed the best intentions of individuals and groups.

6) **The lower-level, capitalist-supporting elite:** This is a very small class which has no revolutionary potential. It includes people who make six-figure annual salaries as managers of banks, individual factories, or large-scale, profit-making, corporate workplaces. It also includes many, although not all, members of Congress, state government and large local governments, and those appointed to top-level Cabinet or Cabinet-type positions or their state and local equivalents. In addition, members of this class run TV and radio stations and major newspapers, run pro-capitalist think tanks and ruling-class research and policy-developing institutions, and are top administrators of major colleges and universities.

These are the public faces of the usually behind-the-scenes ruling class. A small number of the individual members of this class may believe that they are good people only being "realistic" about the system and doing their best to administer their part of it in a "humane" way. They are unable to see the forest for the trees. Trapped within the logic of major capitalist institutions and the capitalist value system and method of operations, whatever good works they accomplish are a small drop or two in a sea of tears.

Some of these people may wheel and deal or get lucky and move up to the top, ruling-class level. Indeed, many have this objective in mind and look for opportunities to maximize their wealth or power so as to achieve this goal.

They are a group not to be trusted. If an individual member of this class decides to break ranks—Dan Ellsberg of "Pentagon Papers" fame and former Attorney-General Ramsey Clark come to mind—they should be welcomed and encouraged to continue growing and changing for the better, but as a class this group is poison and clearly deserving of the description, "the enemy." (When I say "enemy" I mean as a class, not on individual terms. The goal of revolutionary transformation cannot be the elimination of the individuals but the elimination of a class, a social/economic category determined by what a particular group of individuals do.) In a new society this class would have no place; it would be replaced by democratically-chosen managers and leaders. Until that day comes, there can be no confusion about the reality of this grouping as impediments, obstacles, barricades in the way of fundamental social transformation.

7) **The corporate/financial ruling class**: enemy numero uno. These are the major shareholders and owners of the Fortune 500 corporations and banks, the Rockefellers, Duponts, Hunts, Fords, Mellons, Trumps, Gettys, and their ilk. They are not a well-known group; they generally prefer to remain out of the public eye, with some exceptions. They have accumulated their wealth in virtually every case as a result of massive and crippling exploitation of people and the natural environment. They control government through large campaign contributions, outright bribes, the use of the mass media, and similar means. They are responsible for U.S. imperial and militaristic wars, occupations and semi-occupations throughout the world. They consciously confuse, if not outright control, the minds of far too many working-class and middle-class people about the nature of this society and the options to it through their ownership of the mass media. They have major influence over the nation's elite educational institutions.

This is a very tiny group; no more than 1/2 of 1% of the population and, at its core, even less. Yet it owns over 42% of the wealth of the society, about the same amount as the bottom 90% of the population. Hundreds of millions of people around the world are living miserable lives because of this group's greed, power and violence.

Until this class is removed from power, major chunks of its wealth redistributed to its rightful owners—those who suffered, or whose family members suffered in the past, so that these rulers could achieve obscene levels of wealth and power—and steps begun to dissolve this class as a class, there can be no hope for a just, peaceful, democratic and environmentally healthy world.

Working Class Unity or Popular Alliance?

What does all this mean as far as the question of strategy?

First, we need to reaffirm the realities of class exploitation as central to the system. More specifically, we need to reject strategic perspectives which downplay the importance of the working class because the industrial working class, in actual numbers, is declining and becoming less able to lead the general working-class struggle for social progress. We must also reject the argument which says that because class oppression, in the traditional sense of the term, is of declining significance, supposedly, in today's economy, the correct approach to take is to just bring together all the various sectors of the population who are or will be putting forward progressive demands for change, without prioritizing class as a key element within that alliance.

Even though industrial workers are no longer a major portion of the workforce, virtually all workers in various categories of work continue to experience exploitation of their labor. Workers suffer from the fragmentation of the work process. They are often forced to work at stressful, boring or dangerous jobs that are one small part of an overall set of fragmented tasks divided up among many workers. Additionally, in the words of labor analyst Kim Moody, "The end point of the new production systems, in both goods-producing and service-producing sectors, is a growing number of part-time, temporary and contract jobs which now compose a third of the workforce in the U.S. and over half the new employment created each year." (2) The average annual income for workers has been going down, in real terms, over the past 20 years.

Within the overall 70-80% of the population that makes up the working class, all three sectors of that class—the barely-surviving, the low-income and the moderate/middle-income sectors—are important to the alliance that must be built, but it is the low-income, working-class sector that is both the largest numerically and, for various reasons, most consistently progressive, open to anti-capitalist consciousness, and

-46-

capable of engaging in effective action.

One major reason for the strategic importance of the low-income, working-class sector is, of course, its low income. It is an historic fact that economic difficulties are a primary motivation for people to become active in movements to improve their lives. No revolution has ever taken place because masses of people living reasonably well decided that things could be done better and then went about the process of making things change.

However, economic difficulty <u>alone</u> is not sufficient to move masses of people into action. This is why the "barely surviving" has generally not been a <u>consistent</u> vanguard sector for fundamental change within society. More is needed; and part of the "more" for the low-income working class is the experience of being <u>collectively</u> exploited or abused on the job and learning the lessons of collective organization. Even with the low rates of union organization within U.S. society today, workers on the job have other ways of joining together to "watch one another's back" or make the eight hours (or ten or twelve) on the job go more easily.

Another major reason for the strategic importance of this sector is the reality that a large majority of the women workers and workers of color in the U.S. workforce are to be found here. The dual or triple oppressions of class/race, gender/class, or class/race/gender, are powerful teaching tools about the true nature of the system.

Yet the most powerful movements of the past half a century in the U.S. have <u>not</u> been the labor movement, or a conscious working-class movement. Instead, those movements have been the African American movement, the student and anti-Vietnam war movements, the women's movement, the anti-nuclear and peace movements, the environmental movement and the lesbian/gay rights movement. Within many of those movements working-class people have been a major, if not majority, component, and individual working-class and labor people have played leading roles. But a movement of the working class as a class <u>for itself</u> and its needs has not been seen in this country since the CIO upsurge of the 1930s and '40s.

Hopefully this will change one day soon. It is certainly the case that all over the country workers at a grassroots level are organizing in committed and often creative ways to develop new forms of organization and against oppressive bosses. A "new voice" AFL-CIO leadership was elected in late

'95 and has shown some signs, even if inconsistent, of having both a new voice <u>and</u> a new commitment to a different kind of labor movement. A slowly-growing number of unions are beginning to organize <u>across national borders</u>, particularly with Mexican workers following the passage of NAFTA. And in June, 1996 an historic convention in Cleveland, Ohio founded a first-ever U.S. Labor Party.

Yet U.S. history, especially recent history, argues for the "popular alliance" approach rather than a "unite the working class" approach as the most sound strategy to follow to advance the progressive movement toward fundamental social transformation.

But it's not really an either/or situation. The fact is that the best possibilities for uniting the working class itself lie with the popular alliance strategy. Both are important; and both are concretely interconnected.

The major divisions keeping the working class separated are racism and sexism. If a popular alliance emerges that unites the movements of people of color, the women's movement, the progressive elements of the labor movement and other working-class based (e.g., community) movements, there is an <u>arena for popular education</u> on these and other divisive ideologies. In the process of working together around commonly felt issues of concern, people grow and change. This can only benefit the working class.

A popular alliance will be of benefit to the progressive trade unions that continue to contend with middle-of-the-road to conservative elements within their ranks. By putting forward its program for resolution of the crises of U.S. society, by organizing around that program and in support of its immediate demands on the government, by running candidates for office on that program, masses of working-class people both inside and outside of the trade union movement can be educated and galvanized into action. This can only help the process of trade union organization and working-class-based community organization.

Of course, in order for these positive developments to take place out of the alliance-building process, it is important that there be significant involvement of working-class leaders in the leadership of the alliance. There will be other classes part of the alliance—farmers, professionals, small businesspeople, ministers, others. In the absence of a conscious commitment to have a broadly-based, multi-racial leadership representing not just the different movements and sectors of the population but also the different sectors of the working class, the potential of the alliance will not be realized.

It is also critical that the alliance, over time, take the form of an independent political party.

Footnotes for Chapter 4

1) Harry Braverman, "The Making of the U.S. Working Class," Monthly Review, November, 1994

2) Kim Moody, "Pulled Apart, Pushed Together," Crossroads Magazine, October, 1994

DOWN WITH THE TWO
CORPORATE-DOMINATED PARTIES

In order for there to be positive social change that benefits the vast majority of the population of the United States, as well as the world, it is essential that the popular alliance takes the form of an independent political party, an alternative to the Democratic and Republican parties dominated by and part of the existing system.

This is not exactly an original thought. As long ago as 1886, Frederick Engels, referring to the United States, spoke of how "the first great step of importance for every country newly entering into the movement is always the constitution of the workers as an independent political party, no matter how, so long as it is a distinct workers' party." (1)

Throughout U.S. history there have been movements which have developed into mass-based parties independent of the Democrats and Republicans. Indeed, the modern-day, two-party system was born in the 1850s and 1860s when the Whig Party split over the issue of slavery, giving birth to the Republican Party. Abraham Lincoln was elected President in 1860 with less than 40% of the popular vote because there were three candidates for President, the Democrat, the Republican and the Whig.

Over time the Whig Party disappeared and the Democrat/Republican duopoly came to be enshrined as the method of political rule by the dominant economic forces. However, throughout this period of time, there have been periodic, organized, mass efforts to create alternatives.

In the 1880s and 1890s a strong populist movement, based in the rural areas of the South and Midwest, emerged which gave birth to the People's Party. By the mid-'90s, this party had developed a following of anywhere from 25-45% of the electorate in twenty states.

Following the demise of the Peoples Party, the second decade of the 1900s saw the development of a growing Socialist Party. During the Presidential election of 1920, its Presidential candidate, Eugene Debs, received 6% of the vote.

During the 1930s the upper midwest experienced strong, independent, Farmer-Labor Parties which won a number of electoral campaigns, including the governorship of Minnesota.

In the late '40s Henry Wallace ran as the Progressive Party candidate for President. Although in the early stages of his campaign against Democrat Harry Truman and Republican Tom Dewey he was polling 15-20% of the vote, Wallace ended up with about one million votes as Truman rhetorically moved to the left, coopting and absorbing Wallace's base of support.

Also in the '40s and into the early '50s, the American Labor Party in New York City successfully elected Vito Marcantonio to the U.S. Congress from East Harlem six times and played a significant role in the political life of the city.

In the mid-'60s, as part of the upsurge of the African American freedom movement, the Lowndes County, Alabama Freedom Party, the National Democratic Party of Alabama and the Mississippi Freedom Democratic Party briefly emerged as black-led, working-class-based independent alternatives.

And yet, here we are at the beginning of the 21st century, and there is neither a broadly-based, visible mass workers' party nor a peoples' party uniting various popular movements and sectors. Why is this?

Many of the reasons have been addressed previously: the strength of individualism and pro-capitalist ideology, racism and racial division within the working class and among the population as a whole, the wealth generated by the capitalist system which was grudgingly "shared" by the powers-that-be, allowing a significant percentage of the working class to achieve middle-income status, and the strength of reformism as a conscious or unconscious approach to organizing. Repression against the Left, organizations based in communities of color, the labor movement and other progressive groups has also been a major factor.

In addition, the method of operation of the Democratic Party has had much to do with this problem.

The Democratic Party is a strategic instrument of the ruling elite to continue their rule. They have perfected its methods of operation over decades. During periods of mass upsurge, as during the 1890s, the 1930s or the 1960s, it acts as a lightning rod to attract dissenting or resisting movements and absorb them like a sponge, draining their vitality and taming them so that they ultimately sputter and die, choked of their dynamism and energy. It accepts as much reform as necessary, but as little as possible, in order to calm the people's anger, coopt the people's leaders, and ride out the storm. Then, when the crisis has passed, it gradually curtails those reforms and cuts back programs in the peoples' interest. In periods of popular apathy, the Democratic Party takes on a conservative hue, and then takes on a pinkish coloration as grass-roots movements inevitably emerge and begin making radical demands. The political stance of the Democratic Party is a kind of litmus paper of the strength of the peoples' movements.

The most recent example of this process is what happened with the 1980s Jesse Jackson/Rainbow Coalition movement.

From 1983 to 1987 Jackson and the Rainbow were essentially an independent force, operating within the Democratic Party but with mechanisms of decision-making outside the dominant circles of that party. The Rainbow was in essence a coalition between a number of left-wing Democrats, particularly African Americans, and independent progressive activists outside the Party structures. For most of that period of time, the need that Jackson and the left-wing Democrats had for the energies and commitment of the independents meant that the Rainbow organization, by and large, was independent.

By late 1987, however, Jackson and his inner circle of advisors had decided to bring into his second Presidential campaign a number of establishment Democratic Party operatives. They also cut back on the resources available for the more-independent Rainbow Coalition structure. Prior to the Democratic Convention in Atlanta in 1988, Democratic Party stalwart Ron Brown was put in charge of the Jackson campaign's operations during the Convention.

One of the major focuses of the Jackson campaign in Atlanta was on the Democratic Party's platform. Because of this focus, and <u>because of the method of operation of the Democratic Party in periods of mass progressive upsurge</u>, a platform was adopted that <u>was</u> progressive, by and large. The candidate nominated that year, however, Michael Dukakis, did not campaign on the basis of that platform until the last couple of weeks of his campaign when he was so far behind George Bush that he figured he had nothing to lose. At that point he began to use similar rhetoric to that Jackson had used during the primaries, but it was too little, too late to have enough of an impact, and Bush won.

Jackson's response in the midst of this situation was to squash independent Rainbow organizing which was taking place in many parts of the country throughout 1988. State Rainbow organizations which had taken the initiative to organize state Rainbow conferences to plan for future action following the July Atlanta Democratic Convention were directed

<u>not</u> to do so. This directive was then capped off at a March, 1989 meeting of the Rainbow's National Board where Jackson, running and dominating the meeting, rammed through a restructuring proposal brought in by nine of 15 members of a restructuring commission he had appointed in December 1988. A minority proposal from the other six members of the commission was unilaterally determined as unnecessary by Jackson and was not even presented for consideration. At the same time, the composition of the National Board was changed to exclude most independents and include more Democrats.

Ever since, Jackson has been a loyal Democrat, and the National Rainbow has become a shell of its former self. And, surprise of surprises, the Democratic Party has moved steadily rightwards. A classic case of retreat, coopt, undercut and, as a result, continue to rule.

Another reason for the absence of an effective, mass-based, independent political party has to do with the nature of the electoral system within the United States.

In most European countries and in many other parts of the world, the electoral system is a parliamentary system in which representatives are elected through some form of proportional representation (PR), where seats are apportioned on the basis of the percentage of votes obtained. In a number of countries, parties which achieve 5% of the vote are able to have representation in national or state legislatures. Usually they receive funding and are in the mass media on a regular basis.

In the U.S.'s winner-take-all system, a political party can achieve as much as 49.9% of the vote in a particular election but obtain no representation in government. This reality encourages unnatural coalitions between progressive people and centrists, and even conservatives, such as is represented by the Democratic Party, in an effort to win elections. Under this winner-take-all system it is much more difficult to build a new party with a clear, popular, progressive program.

There is a growing movement on both the national and international level in support of proportional representation as the most democratic way to elect representatives to government. Most of the world's major democracies use some form of PR, and more are changing their systems of voting into some form of PR every year. Among the countries which use it are: Germany, Sweden, Switzerland, Mexico, New Zealand, Brazil, Russia, Ireland, Israel, Spain, Australia, Italy, Japan, Norway, Finland, Nicaragua, El Salvador and Portugal. Winner-take-all elections are still in place in France, Serbia and Great Britain, although there is growing support for PR there, as well as in some of Britain's former colonies, including the United States, Canada, India, Zimbabwe and some Caribbean islands. (2)

An additional reason for the difficulties faced by progressive-minded candidates is the dominance of the electoral process by big-money interests, the corporate ruling class. Since 1980 this class has tremendously accelerated the amounts of money put into the electoral system to buy and control legislators at all levels. They do this through corporate Political Action Committees, large campaign contributions, lobbying efforts, corporate-controlled "citizens' organizations" used in a variety of ways to affect legislation before Congress or state and local governments, or outright bribes, suitably disguised or hidden. This has meant that for most of the people running for office from both major parties, it is extremely difficult to run for office and win without compromising basic principles. The higher up you go in the electoral arena, the more difficult it is to avoid being sucked in to the system's corruption.

An additional reason for this state of affairs has to do with the weaknesses of the U.S. Left. Primary among them is the strength of "lesser of two evils" ideology.

This unwillingness to break with the Democratic Party is also related to the reality that for unions, community organizations, issue-based organizations or any group trying to defend the rights or incomes of its members or to achieve some kind of change, sooner or later it is necessary to deal with the government to try to convince or force them to accede to your demands. Particularly in periods in which independent mass activity is at a low ebb, it is hard to avoid dealing with Democrats (and Republicans) in efforts to achieve those demands. The temptation is very strong to tone down the demands, to build friendly relationships with people, usually Democrats, who say they believe in the same things you do but are just being "realistic." This is a very seductive process into which even the best of people can be absorbed.

However, today neither the Republicans nor the Democrats have anywhere near as many "goodies" to dole out as in the past. Two-party government these days doles out more budget cuts and bad news than they do programs to meet people's needs. And this reality shows no signs of changing without a massive people's movement which is determined to reverse the direction of the country.

Some groups have looked at this set of realities and determined that the place to focus attention is on reform of the electoral system. A grass-roots movement is emerging to change our electoral system so that proportional representation—representation based not on winner-take-all but on a more fair reflection of actual vote totals—becomes the U.S. method of choosing government representatives. This is an essential part of the process of bringing about change in this country. Unless we can change the electoral rules, making it much more possible for grassroots and progressive candidates to run and win, it will be extremely difficult to build up the critical mass of independent candidacies and victories that are necessary for a broadly-based and effective independent party to emerge.

Other groups are attempting to change state laws so that candidates can run on both a major party line and a new, independent party line at the same time. This is a kind-of half-way house for those Democrats who want to move in an independent direction but are afraid of stepping out too far. This "fusion" approach can be useful, but it can also be implemented in a way that builds an organization dependent upon Democratic Party personalities rather than the building of independent, progressive political organization. Those who have posed this fusion approach as the central objective of a "new party" effort are skating on very thin ice.

It is essential that reforms be made to take big, corporate money out of the electoral system, with the most radical—and most democratic—proposal being to virtually eliminate private donations above $100 and go to a system of public, government funding to candidates who can demonstrably show a base of support. Unless the stranglehold over the electoral system by big money can be seriously reduced, it will be very difficult for an independent party to emerge and eventually build up the strength to contend for power.

These and other reforms make sense as goals to work toward and as reforms to try to implement even under the fundamentally undemocratic system we now have. However, it is hard to see how any of these objectives, to any significant degree, will happen absent a major change in the political dynamics within the country, i.e., without an independent mass movement that crystalizes into the form of an independent party.

There is an additional reason why a mass political party, an alternative to the Democrats and Republicans, is a necessary form for an independent, progressive movement serious about fundamental social change in the United States.

This is not Russia, Nicaragua, El Salvador, South Africa, Haiti or China. The United States is a country in which "democratic" elections have been the method of choosing government leaders going back to George Washington. The fact that those elections have been distorted by the influence of big money, increasingly so today, or the fact that women until the 1920s and African Americans in the South until the 1960s could not vote, does not change the political reality that it has been electoral campaigns, not military coups or armed revolts, that have been the historic method of determining those people who will steer the ship of state. This dynamic is deeply rooted in the collective political psyche of the U.S. population.

Accordingly, if we on the Left wish to build a mass movement for systemic change, we cannot avoid the necessity of constructing an electoral-oriented political party that will represent and be based upon the popular alliance. Once such a party has been created, and as it helps to strengthen mass movement around a number of issues because of the changed political dynamics in the country which will come about in part because of its existence and its work, more and more people will come to see the limitations of a solely electoral party and be open to other, more direct forms of political struggle. Indeed, one of our tasks is to work to build a new progressive party that is not just electoral but also issue-oriented, that works throughout the year and not just at election time. Without this extra-electoral work, this movement-building, our new progressive party will become less and less progressive as individuals out to make a political career for themselves within the party assert their dominance.

It is likely that, in the short term, this "party" will take the form of a coalition of several parties which have been developing during the decade of the '90s. But such a coalition will really be, to broad numbers of people, an alternative party in fact and, over time, it is to be desired and expected that this coalition will function more like an actual unitary party, even if it continues as an alliance of several different groups.

We need to recognize that this new party will include people who come from the left-wing of the Democratic Party, as well as independents who have been influenced by the model of politics practiced by most Democratic and Republican politicians. Some of these people are good on the issues and are conscientious about truly serving the people. Others may be good on the issues but have been influenced by the system's corrupt ways of operating such that there will be a need for conscious efforts to ensure that the new party operates on the basis of full-scale democracy, political independence and accountability of leadership.

There are three major aspects to the process of building towards a mass-based, independent political party today.

1) It is critical that we run candidates on "third party" lines and build up independent organizational forms engaged in grass-roots organizing around the issues affecting working people. We need candidates willing to stand up and be crystal clear about their allegiance to the interests of the people and not the corporate-dominated parties, able to demonstrate that there is a base of voting support for independent candidacies. As much as possible there should be connections between the electoral and the non-electoral activity. Building these two-pronged forms of independent organization is essential, strategic work.

2) As indicated above, we must also be about the process of changing the electoral rules-of-the-game. We must change our undemocratic winner-take-all system to one whereby proportional representation is used in the election of government officials. We need to take big money out of the political process and move toward public financing of elections. These are the two electoral reforms that can do the most to open up the political system to those who have been historically disenfranchised.

3) At the same time, we must pay careful attention to the struggle within the Democratic Party and maintain our connections with those willing to work with us and support our demands and programs. Strategically, we must build unity of action with the forces inside the Democratic Party who are open to or moving towards independence. We have to recognize that it will be difficult to build a broad, national independent party without the active involvement of a growing number of these people.

These three aspects are mutually dependent. If we fail to carry out our specifically independent tasks, running candidates and organizing around issues, there will be no pole toward which those forces moving towards independence within the Democratic Party will gravitate. If we do not change the electoral rules-of-the-game, it will be hard to build up the critical mass of electoral victories that any mass electoral movement and party needs to attract growing support. At the same time, if we do not build unity of action with the best of the progressive forces within the Democratic Party, it will be difficult to reform the electoral process, and we will be relatively isolated and unlikely of long-term success.

We need to look for those races where independents can run, clearly distinguish themselves from both Republicans and Democrats and make a strong showing. It does not make sense, certainly at this beginning stage of independent mass party development, to run against genuinely progressive Democrats whose positions on issues are good and who have generally healthy relationships with progressive and grassroots organizations in their district.

The bottom line for all of this electoral work, however, is that just as it is a form of work which we must take up and engage in wherever it makes sense, as independents, there are very real dangers associated with it. In the absence of collective organizational forms to keep candidates honest, serious problems can easily develop during a campaign or after a person wins office, or becomes a prominent person as a result of the campaign.

Our objective in this work is not the advancement of the political careers of movement "stars." Our objective is the economic, social and cultural transformation of society into one which is truly about justice and liberation for all people. The running of candidates, and the establishment and building of an independent political party, are means to an end, not the end. The question which we then need to examine more specifically is: what kind of a new society do we have in mind that we are working towards?

Footnotes

1) Frederick Engels, "A Letter to Friedrich Sorge," November, 1886, quoted in Letters to Americans, International Publishers, p. 163

2) "Government Of, By and For the People," prepared by the Center for Voting and Democracy, Washington, D.C.

A NEW SOCIETY:
WHAT WOULD IT LOOK LIKE?*

The development of capitalism in Europe and the world-wide colonial system emerging out of it has been responsible for tremendous human misery and environmental destruction. Yet the fact is that with the wealth, industry, technology and scientific knowledge of humankind as it has developed, we are clearly capable of providing an adequate, if not decent, standard of living for everyone in the world. Planning will be necessary; steps must be taken quickly to deal with serious environmental damage which is already beginning to have significant impacts worldwide; the rapid rate of growth in population which threatens to undercut progressive social and economic policies must be dealt with through widespread education and family planning efforts, in combination with people-oriented, sustainable economic development; but it seems difficult to deny that the material prerequisites are present to create a very different type of new society.

There is also reason to believe that these economic changes would be accompanied by social and cultural changes that will allow for a much fuller and wider flowering of human creativity, personal and spiritual development and scientific exploration. In a society governed by principles of social and economic justice and a much fairer distribution of wealth and power, all members of society, not just the well-off elite, would have less "work pressure," more time and more opportunities to pursue non-work interests.

What would the defenders of our existing economic system have to say about this "utopian" vision of a new society?

---

*There are many other aspects to a new society that need to be envisioned and discussed than are raised in this chapter, among them: how schools teach in a way which creates new generations of non-elitist, democratic and independent-thinking young people; the future of religious institutions and the role of spirituality; the nature of loving/family relationships in a non-patriarchal, non-homophobic society; the fundamental changes necessary such that production processes are non-polluting and earth-friendly; and the role of cultural institutions, both traditional and newly-developing, in relationship to the process of social transformation. Space considerations, however, allow for only a more limited focus on economic questions in this chapter.

The essential difference between capitalist and socialist society, theoretically, is that under capitalism, society is seen as progressing forward as individuals strive to increase their personal wealth, regardless of the impact upon other human beings, within certain socially- and governmentally-prescribed (and changing) limits. At its most reactionary, its proponents argue the so-called human nature argument; i.e., that human beings have always been primarily motivated by greed and desire for wealth and that "you can't change human nature." At its more progressive, the argument made is that entrepreneurial energy, unfettered by undue government control, is the fuel which motivates invention, fresh thinking, new technologies, and economic advance.

Under socialism, on the other hand, the needs of society are advanced through a process of public ownership of the productive forces, rational planning as to what those institutions produce, and a just distribution of the products so as to consciously benefit all members of society.

However, given the experiences of "really existing socialism" in the Soviet Union, China and elsewhere over the past 83 years, the capitalist critique of socialism cannot be brushed aside so easily.

Albert Einstein, in "Why Socialism," first published in 1949 in Monthly Review magazine, succinctly posed the problem: "It is necessary to remember that a planned economy is not yet socialism. A planned economy as such may be accompanied by the complete enslavement of the individual. The achievement of socialism requires the solution of some extremely difficult socio-political problems: how is it possible, in view of the far-reaching centralization of political and economic power, to prevent bureaucracy from becoming all-powerful and overweening? How can the rights of the individual be protected and therewith a democratic counterweight to the power of bureaucracy be assured?"

Einstein's observations ring true for those of us who have seen the Soviet Union fall apart from its own internal contradictions (contradictions mightily aggravated by the conscious efforts of capitalism to subvert and destroy it), or who, long before the demise of the USSR, did not look to this first attempt to build socialism as a model to emulate for the U.S.A. It is an historic fact that going back as far as the 1920s there were serious deformations in the Soviet model which, over time, became more and more serious.

The Soviet Union's demise accelerated a process of rethinking among Marxists and revolutionaries around the world in many areas. One of the main areas is the one in question here, which, in essence, boils down to the question of what a transition to a non-capitalist, qualitatively different form of society would look like.

An argument can be made that this new society cannot really be described as socialism. Andre Gorz, a French Marxist, has written of how the advancement of industry and technology, particularly the processes of automation that have made an eight-hour work day increasingly redundant and unnecessary in social terms, raises the issue of what kind of new society is envisioned? "There are two basic alternatives: fully 'programmed'. . ., technocratic societies, or a liberated society, which Marx called 'communist,' in which the necessary production of necessities occupies only a small part of everyone's time and where (waged) work ceases to be the main activity. . . Waged work cannot remain the centre of gravity or even the central activity in our lives. Any politics which denies this, whatever its ideological pretensions, is a fraud." (1)

Gorz makes an important point. It is not sufficient that our vision of a new society be confined solely to the world of "waged work." It is not enough that instead of being told by all-powerful bosses and managers what to do, we can democratically choose our managers and have more say over what we do on the job, as important as that will be.

A good deal of what workers, professionals and managers "do" under advanced capitalist society would not be done in a different kind of society. There would be no need for the millions of people producing armaments for the military, and serving in the military. The financial services industry, which exists for the primary purpose of helping people with money to make more money, including a tremendous amount of unproductive speculation, would undergo major downsizing, as would the real estate, advertising, insurance and banking industries. All of these are tremendously bloated beyond what is necessary in a rational and people-oriented, non-capitalist economy. And these examples could certainly be multiplied.

Yet, in the words of Barbara Ehrenreich, in the immediate transitional period from capitalism to a truly liberating society, "there is so much to do. If profit were not the principle guiding human endeavor, we could easily employ a couple of generations just cleaning up the mess: salvaging the environment, curing disease, educating the ignorant, housing the homeless. Once that is done, we might throw ourselves en masse into the great adventures of scientific inquiry, artistic expression, and space exploration." (2)

Gorz' point is not necessarily in contradiction to Ehrenreich's. Gorz is talking about <u>alienated</u> wage labor; Ehrenreich is talking about socially necessary work. In the long run, Gorz is right; capitalism has advanced the wealth and knowledge of human society, in <u>economic</u> terms, such that the possibilities for moving beyond this exploitative system are very real, in a material sense. Ehrenreich, conversely, draws our attention to the many kinds of socially useful, and, for that matter, personally fulfilling (potentially) forms of work that must accompany any process of transition to a liberating society.

But we are still left with some major questions, among them: will all economic institutions be owned by the government, nationalized, and/or publicly controlled? Is there a place for private ownership of business within a liberating society?

Let's begin this discussion by returning to Marx.

Marx was right about some things and wrong about others. One of the things he was right about was that capitalism would develop the productive forces to the point at which the age-old problem of material scarcity would be transcended, and it would be possible to meet the material needs of all because of the advance of industry and technology. We are at that point now, and it makes no sense to go backwards, dismantling what is potentially liberating. The need is to develop the appropriate mix of forms of ownership and control such that humanity is able to live decently with the natural environment in proper balance, with democracy, social justice and equality as fundamental motivating principles and increasing realities.

There are differing views among socialists and Marxists about what this should mean. Some, of course, continue to believe that government ownership, centralized planning, and some degree of democratic involvement consistent with them, is the way to go. Others have a more flexible approach.

Ralph Milliband, a prominent Marxist, insists that "the point is not to nationalize everything in sight, which is an absurd and destructive notion, but to create a 'mixed economy' in which the public sector is predominant—in other words, to reverse the present arrangements where it is the private sector which is overwhelmingly predominant. . . As for the market, the question is not whether it should exist, but how large should be its role. Socialism means, among other things, that cash, the ability to pay, is not the means of access to health, education and much else on which civilized life depends. It means, in other words, a progressive decommodification of life, the removal of the cash nexus as the core of social relations." (3)

It's hard to consider yourself a socialist unless you believe that some forms of public ownership are necessary. After all, the problems and crises of capitalist society stem from the <u>private</u> ownership of industry and finance by a tiny minority of ultra-rich white men.

In recent years, the necessity of <u>democracy</u> in the running of a socialist system has become an article of faith for most revolutionaries.

And finally, the necessity of the use of "the market," or, more to the point (and not really what capitalists have in mind when they talk about "the market"), the actual social demand for a particular product in determining what products are created, how they are modified, how many are produced, and what price is charged, is also fairly widely accepted.

The key issue, however, boils down to the question of ownership and control of the major industrial and financial institutions of society. With this control comes the massive and obscene use of big business profits for individual gain, while, even in the best of circumstances, workers within the individual enterprise are exploited on the job and receive a fraction of the wealth they create. Very often they receive wages that are barely enough or not enough to meet basic survival needs.

With ownership and control comes the ability to determine where to invest the business profits, what products to make, what branches to shut down or move overseas, etc., all of which can have major social and environmental impacts.

If one is committed to the emergence of a truly <u>liberating</u> society, one in which the wealth of society created by the work of the vast majority is put at the disposal of that vast majority to determine, democratically, how it should best be used, it is impossible to reconcile the private ownership of the industries and financial institutions most directly responsible for the production of this wealth with that objective. The major corporations must become owned and controlled by a combination of the workers in those institutions and the consuming public which buys the products. Government, in some form or other, must also be involved in this process to ensure that the interests of the entire society and the environment are adequately represented in the decision-making processes and in the use of the wealth created.

To the extent possible, there should be decentralization of ownership and control to maximize democratic input and involvement and guard against bureaucratic blockages and obstructions. For example, when it comes to the production of food, the land presently owned by agribusiness corporations should be broken down into smaller, manageable, farmer cooperatives, with farmers who have been forced off the land, or workers for agribusiness, given the first opportunity to become coop members. Perhaps some of the farmland would be sold back to individual farm families, with provisions, and technical assistance, to encourage coopera-tion with others and the most efficient and environmentally sound farming techniques. Over time, it is to be expected that the best possible size and method of farmer cooperatives would be determined from practice and experience. And the validity of individual land ownership in relationship to the egalitarian objectives of the overall liberating society could be determined.

Another example is car production. What if General Motors became an employee-owned business, with workers democratically choosing the leadership of the business, in a way similar to the best of democratic union elections for union leadership? That leadership, in turn, would be responsible for the selection and overseeing of management, with local leadership choosing local management and national leadership choosing management responsible for overall national coordination, planning and relations with representatives of the consuming public and government. Ultimate decision-making, on local and national levels, might rest with leadership bodies made up of representatives of the employee/owner's association, the union (which would still be necessary to deal with specifically labor/management problems), consumers/ community and the government.

Due to the initiative of one of these sectors, a decision might be made that instead of producing gasoline-powered automobiles, production processes should be revamped to allow for the production of environmen-tally-friendly, solar-powered automobiles. In the process of conversion, the workers would have much input into how that process was best effected, since they are in the best position to know how to transform the productive machinery itself most safely and efficiently. This most likely would begin as a local decision by one, or a few, of the automobile plants, although it is possible that due to the environmental consciousness within the population as a whole, and elected officials genuinely in touch with and sharing in that consciousness, the initiative could come from the government or consumer representatives.

And what about banks? Would these be owned by cooperatives of bank employees? Probably not. Money, capital, is central to the capacity of an individual business, and the economy, to survive and grow. Accordingly, this function would best be served by making banks, virtually all banks, publicly owned, democratically controlled, with stringent oversight to insure banking practices consistent with the goals of the new society. Allowing individuals or cooperatives of workers to own banks will open up possibilities for profit-taking and speculation. As we saw in the 1980s with the multi-billion-dollar Savings and Loan scandal, this is a very bad idea. It is inconsistent with the principles of a liberating society.

Some of these approaches toward big, monopoly businesses could also be applied toward medium-sized businesses. The key principles would be:

- cooperative ownership and control by the workers within the business, with provisions for consumer and government representation;

- democratic methods and forms of governance in the process of decision-making;

- safe and clean workplaces with respect for the rights of workers and for the environment;

- a dramatic narrowing of the extremes of income between top-level management and lower-level workers. In some businesses within capitalist society the highest paid CEO makes hundreds of times as much money as does the lowest-paid, full-time employee. This is fundamentally unjust;

- concern for the social and environmental impact of what is produced; willingness to convert to other uses if necessary.

How would these kinds of transformations take place?

To a very limited extent some of them have already begun. In communities across the country workers, unions, local government officials, religious leaders and other community representatives have joined together to form coalitions for "industrial retention and renewal." These coalitions have emerged over the past 15 years as major corporations have laid off hundreds, thousands or tens of thousands of workers at a shot, decimating entire communities in the process. In some cases workers, with community support, have been able to retain some industry, and some jobs, through unified, cooperative, political efforts.

In addition, there are other worker-owned enterprises. According to the Industrial Cooperative Association in Somerville, Massachusetts, there were a little less than a thousand such companies throughout the country as of the late 1980s.

It is unrealistic in the extreme to think that a new, liberating society is going to emerge through the building up of these alternatives to a point at which the old, dominant capitalist system crumbles and makes way for these alternatives. It will take a political struggle, backed up by various forms of more militant struggle, leading over time to the winning of political and governmental power and the transformation of government as it now exists into a form of government that is genuinely new, qualitatively superior, truly democratic, and popularly-based. Only then will it be possible to begin making these economic transformations on a massive scale. But these small, often heroic efforts at social and economic transformation on local levels today are nevertheless important models from which many others can learn, both positively and negatively, about cooperative possibilities, as well as their limitations under a big business-dominated system.

What about individual ownership of economic institutions? Would it be prohibited in a liberating society?

At the beginning of the process of social transformation, no, without question. For years and decades it can be expected that small, individually-owned businesses will continue to exist and operate. It is not small businesspeople who are the problem. In many ways they can be a part of the solution if they join with workers and others in the popular alliance.

In many cases small businesspeople are workers who are trying to get out from under the control of a boss, make a better living, have more individual freedom, etc. These objectives, in and of themselves, are not problematic; indeed, they are very normal. The problem emerges when small businesspeople become increasingly successful, grow larger, open up new branches, become more detached from personal involvement with the customers, get caught up in the business of making money (as opposed to providing a service) and, as a result, begin to take on some of those same "boss" traits they might have once looked upon with scorn and anger.

Clearly, size of business, and extent of individual income and wealth, will need to be regulated in a liberating society. Most likely, limitations will have to be placed on the size of individually-owned businesses. In the early years of the transformative process the size allowed will be larger than can be expected to be the case later. Indeed, as the process of social transformation proceeds, increasing numbers of people, <u>including many individual owners themselves</u>, will come to believe in the economic soundness, the secureness, of the new society unfolding before their eyes. As a result they will develop a more cooperative and social-oriented consciousness and conscience, which in turn will probably lead them to look for other forms of work more in keeping with that consciousness. Or they may come up with ways of improving their business to make it more humane and consumer-friendly.

In other words, not through coercion, not through violence, not through bureaucracy, but through a change in worldview, a change in one's heart, if you will, capitalist ideology will begin to die away and liberating, socially responsible ideology will flower and grow in the soil of an economic/social system which ensures that the human needs of all are the top-most priority of the institutions of society, including the government.

Government! What about government? What is its role in this process of forging a liberating society?

Government is a necessary evil. Even the most benevolent government exists for the purpose of "keeping order," of ensuring that individual members of society obey the laws and rules of that society. Even under a government that is about the process of social transformation, some people, a small capitalist minority, would experience coercive action to deprive them of their obscene wealth and dangerous power, to prevent them from causing any more human and environmental damage.

Under capitalist society, government's primary role is to maintain the unjust status quo based upon racism, sexism, class oppression, homophobia and other forms of inequality. Both parties, Democrats and Republicans, are about this task. There are differences between them as to <u>how</u> to do so, with the Republicans generally being more up-front with their efforts to benefit big business and the historic beneficiaries of institutionalized privilege. Some Democrats try to enact reforms that give working and low-income people more opportunities and more wealth under capitalism, but very few are willing to challenge the injustice of the system itself. And the willingness of most politicians to work for progressive reforms is almost always a function of mass pressure from below, from the grassroots.

During periods when the ruling corporate class feels threatened by a rising popular movement, government's role is to coopt or, if necessary, divide and destroy that movement. In the 20th century in the United States we have seen this happen in a major way during the period after World War I (the Palmer Raids, the imprisonment of Eugene Debs, mass deportations and jailings), after World War II (the McCarthy period, attacks on the CIO, Smith Act prosecutions) and during the 1960s and early '70s (numerous conspiracy trials, the FBI's Cointelpro program against Martin Luther King, Jr., the Black Panther Party, and other organizations of people of color, widespread infiltration and disruption of progressive groups).

On an international level, the United States government, since World War II, has played the role of global policeman, violently attempting to beat down efforts on the part of colonized nations or popular movements to obtain national independence and social justice for their countries.

Of course, government under capitalism performs basic governmental functions as well: building and maintaining roads, bridges, railroads and other infrastructure; providing for public education; social services of some kind, the extent of which is determined primarily by the strength and visibility of mass movements demanding them; regulation of conflicts between the demands of business and the greater public good in cases where there is broad public support for governmental action, e.g., as regards environmental protection; and other such functions. These are functions that, to one degree or another, government has performed for decades in countries around the world.

In recent years, government has been consciously reduced as far as its regulatory and social service roles as the Fortune 500 use their immense wealth and power to bring into office elected officials willing to do their bidding. Walter Wriston, past chairman of Citicorp and spokesperson for major sections of the transnational corporate class, has written in his book, The Twilight of Sovereignty, "Money is asserting its control over (government), disciplining irresponsible policies and taking away free lunches everywhere." International traders take "a vote on the soundness of each country's fiscal and monetary policies" and this "giant vote-counting machine conducts a running tally on what the world thinks of a government's diplomatic, fiscal and monetary policies and this opinion is immediately reflected in the value the market places on a country's currency." He goes on to state that "capital goes where it is wanted and stays where it is treated well." (4)

The successful bribery and arm-twisting by President Bill Clinton in the early '90s to obtain passage of NAFTA, and the subsequent passage of GATT, only confirm this lessening of the power of government, or, indeed, the cozying up of government to corporate power.

There is a need for a counterweight to corporate power. Mass organization, mass movements, an independent political party are all essential parts of that counter-weight, but these are limited as long as the control of government is in the hands of those who are hostile to, or benignly neglectful of, at best, the interests of working-class people, the environment, and social and economic justice. Ultimately the popular alliance, functioning through an electoral party backed up and pushed by mass movement and mass actions, must become the government and begin to enact its program of fundamental changes.

One of the functions of such a government will be to combat the inevitable resistance of the former corporate rulers to the implementation of that program, the lessening and then termination of their power, the taxing away of their obscene wealth. Conscious steps must be taken to prevent the subversion of democracy and the restoration of the old order by those removed from power.

More positively, a liberating government must establish profoundly different ways of electing government leaders and of removing them from office. The control of big money over the political process must be completely eliminated, through public financing of elections, free access for candidates to radio, TV and the print media, and other steps which strengthen democracy. Proportional representation would become the method of electing government representatives in keeping with the commitment to the most broadly-based and broadly-involving democracy. Procedures should be put into place for the recall of elected officials who significantly betray "the public trust." Their salaries should be no higher than, say, two times the average income of working people, and strict limitations on the use of elected office to make money should be enacted, to keep those in office close to the ground and close to the people.

Longer-term, but beginning in embryo right after the acsension to power, conscious steps must be taken to move toward significant decentralization of many functions of government. This was much more difficult in the countries which had socialist-oriented revolutions. The industrial underdevelopment of those countries, combined with the efforts of the capitalist powers to isolate and destroy their historic project, presented what turned out to be insurmountable obstacles to their original visions of a completely new type of society.

It is a different matter in the U.S. The wealth of U.S. society, the advanced level of industry and technology, and the knowledge revolution which almost daily accelerates those processes, will allow for the near-immediate decentralization of many of the things which government does once it is truly "of the people, by the people and for the people."

Indeed, there are United States political realities that make it essential that the alliance government move in this direction. The U.S. has deep-seated, individualist traditions that don't just "question authority" but downright distrust it, traditions going back almost 400 years to the U.S.'s history as a refuge for European religious and political dissenters. There is a healthy skepticism of those in power, a skepticism which can be a positive force and contribute to the process of building a movement for social and economic reconstruction if integrated into the way in which a popular alliance and the many organizations connected to it function.

But we are getting ahead of ourselves. Before we can move to downsize the government in a way which benefits the working class and the population as a whole, it will be necessary to remove the dominant rulers from their positions of wealth and power. There is more discussion needed about the little question of how.

Footnotes

1) Andre Gorz, Paths to Paradise: On the Liberation from Work, South End Press, pps. 32 and 34

2) Barbara Ehrenreich, "Reinventing Abundance," Dollars and Sense, May/June, 1994

3) Ralph Milliband, "Socialism in Question," Monthly Review, March, 1991, p. 23

4) As quoted in Harris and Davidson, "The Cybernetic Revolution and the Crisis of Capitalism," from cy.Rev, July, 1994

ORGANIZATIONAL QUESTIONS

The changes we are talking about are not a minor piece of business. What we are projecting as the necessary alternative to politics and economics as usual can only be described as revolutionary in content.

What, then, about the question of revolutionary organization? Is it possible to have the kinds of changes we are projecting without an organization, or several organizations connected together, of individuals committed to giving their all to make these changes possible?

In my view, forms of revolutionary organization are needed if the changes written about in previous chapters are to take place. Such an organization(s) would have to be made up of people dedicated to working as hard and as conscientiously as possible to understand U.S. society, to learn from past efforts at fundamental, people-oriented change, and to help the U.S. population, especially working-class people, move as quickly as possible towards a new society based on justice, the meeting of human needs and human liberation.

Why is such an organization needed? After all, Marxism and socialism have a checkered history when it comes to this question. More than a few revolutionary organizations, to be charitable, have been and are male-dominated. More than a few have suffered from hierarchical and top-down forms of organization. Far too many have been racist and homophobic. Sectarianism and vanguardism, the substitution of subjective wishes for a realistic assessment of what is possible, have been viruses of often-epidemic proportions among "revolutionary" groups on the Left. Given this history, why are forms of explicitly revolutionary organization necessary?

The one, single, overriding reason has to do with the nature of the enemy we are facing in our struggle for a liberating society. That enemy— the ultra-rich corporate and financial ruling class—is a ruthless and organized enemy. They use their wealth and power within capitalist society to attempt to isolate and/or divide movements of serious opposition to their policies. When necessary, they repress those movements by force if they become too powerful. The most well-known, recent example in our history is the massive campaign, including assassinations, conducted against the civil rights/Black liberation movement of the 1960s.

To deal with such an enemy one essential component is a national organization of dedicated individuals, people deeply rooted within the working class and sections of the middle class, capable of analyzing what steps are necessary to neutralize the power of that ruling elite. Over time, it would play an important role in helping the broader popular alliance and its party achieve the first major objective of winning control of the government so that it can begin to enact its program.

Does this mean that such a revolutionary organization <u>alone</u> is capable of these tasks? No, it does not. There will certainly be other people outside of such an organization who understand the dynamics of power and who will help determine what are the most effective strategies and tactics to use in moving forward on the road towards liberation. But an <u>organization</u> made up of people who have learned through experience and through study about these issues, who collectively devote serious attention to them on a consistent basis, significantly increases the chances for success on the part of the popular alliance.

Would such an organization be a Marxist organization? Probably not, although it is likely that many of its members would consider themselves as at least partially rooted in Marxism. Indeed, the answer to this question is more like "yes and no."

One of Marxism's primary strengths is that it offers a proven <u>method</u> of analyzing social reality. It sees scientific, historical research as essential to a full understanding of a particular phenomenon, set of relationships, social reality, etc. It sees matter, reality, as constantly in motion, evolving, changing, in a dialectical, non-static process. Sociologically, it sees that the struggle for economic survival, the division of society into (economic) classes, and the struggle between contending classes for dominance of society, are the primary motivating forces as far as the <u>economic</u> development of human society (not necessarily its cultural and social development, although it clearly influences them). And it sees the working class as the group which has the ability and potential to transform capitalist society into a qualitatively different form of society, socialism. Socialism, in turn, is seen as a transition to the goal of a classless, government-less, society of abundance unlike any which has ever existed in human history.

To me, these are essential aspects of Marxism that continue to be relevant to us today. There are also many other aspects to the writings of Marx, as well as Engels, Lenin and others who agreed with much of what Marx had to say, which need to be consciously studied as to their relevance.

Yet defining a revolutionary organization as a Marxist organization may well limit its potential, in more ways than one. There are large numbers of people who, over time, might learn from the best of the Marxist tradition but who, for various reasons, have been turned off to groups which call themselves Marxist. Even more significantly, there are insights from other philosophical traditions, particularly feminism, the lesbian/gay rights movement, environmentalism and liberation theology, as well as from communities of color, that must play a key role in shaping the worldview and approach of a new revolutionary organization.

Feminism, for example, has much to teach a mixed revolutionary organization and progressive movement about <u>how</u> to struggle for change in a way that does not replicate the oppressive relationships of the dominant system. Environmentalism brings a crucial critique of polluting industrial society, whether capitalist or "socialist," and the necessity of integrating ecological consciousness into the process of creating a different way of living. The lesbian/gay movement brings the issue of sexuality "out of the closet" and onto the table instead of being repressed and denied; it demands an openness to new ways of thinking about ourselves as not just economic but also sexual beings. Liberation theology reminds us that there is a spiritual aspect to our lives that cannot be overlooked or neglected; indeed, it must be consciously encouraged as part of the process of building up the personal strength to "keep the faith" throughout one's life. Communities of color bring special insights about the connections between politics and culture as well as a challenge to those European-American activists who need to unlearn the Eurocentric, racist worldview which is endemic to U.S. capitalist society.

Traditional Marxist organizations have had weaknesses in one, more than one or even all five of these areas. Accordingly, a new revolutionary organization should take the time to work through questions of interrelation between them and a Marxist perspective. This "working through" process is one of the key tasks of a revolutionary organization, not because it is academically interesting but because it is directly related to the process of forging an alliance capable of challenging for power.

What are other key tasks and roles for a mass-based, alliance-committed, revolutionary group?

A major one was spoken of above. A revolutionary organization must consciously understand all that it can about the U.S. rulers, their methods of rule, the divisions within them, their weaknesses and strengths, their strategies and tactics, so that it can help the popular alliance successfully navigate the dangerous minefields of political struggle for power. It must draw upon the experience of its members, the experience of revolutionaries in other countries down through history, and knowledge gained from serious study so that it can fulfill this function with as few mistakes as possible.

For example, at some point in time when the popular alliance/party has become a reality and is a force which is attracting mass support, the government will send informers and agent provacateurs into the alliance to try to stir up dissension and disunity. Experienced and intelligent people will need to play an active role in combating this divisiveness, investigating the backgrounds of those suspected of "hidden agendas," and determining what are the best ways to either expose them or politically isolate them so that they are ineffective. A revolutionary organization made up of people who have years of experience, as well as young people with vital energy, dedication and commitment, would be in a position to play a valuable role in this process.

On a much deeper and more profound level, a genuinely revolutionary organization would put at the top of its agenda the development of new ways of working together, human interaction at the highest possible levels, cultural change of a pronounced and distinct character. The best insights and experiences out of feminism, liberation theology and communities of color will play a major role in this regard.

This is not solely an internal matter for the revolutionary organization. This work, this process of ideological and cultural change, as we have spoken of earlier, is an essential task for alliance organizers in their interaction with the broader working class and the society as a whole.

Carl Boggs, in his book The Two Revolutions: Gramsci and the Dilemmas of Western Marxixm, wrote of how Italian revolutionary Antonio Gramsci "insisted that bourgeois domination is exercised as much through popular 'consensus' achieved in civil society as through physical coercion (or the threat of it) by the state apparatus, especially in Western capitalist societies where education, mass media, culture and the legal system can so powerfully shape consciousness. The strength of bourgeois forms of hegemony in European countries could be invoked to explain the drift of working-class politics toward moderate reformism and even conservatism. . . Gramsci theorized the possibility of an alternative hegemony, or emergent 'integrated culture,' that would lay the basis of a counter-hegemonic movement broad enough to initiate the transition to socialism. Consistent with the overall premises of Western Marxism, this 'war of position' schema contains two major implications: first, that the transformation of civil society takes on an importance even greater than the contestation for state power and, second, that the new state system must be built upon non-authoritarian foundations." (1)

Gramsci was right on target. In the United States the major reason for the weaknesses and failures of the Left has more to do with the low level of political consciousness on the part of the working class and the general U.S. population, taken as a whole, than it does with anything else. Indeed, this low level of consciousness has been reflected within the organized political Left where the competitive, individualistic, racist and sexist ideology of capitalism has been replicated in many of the various Marxist groupings claiming to be "vanguards" of the working class. Instead of all these groups joining together to increase their effectiveness, there is a long history of sectarianism and turf battles, and minimal leadership from women and people of color.

A new revolutionary organization must be about the ideological and cultural transformation first of itself and, as soon as possible, the broader society. How can we hope to be looked to for leadership if the ways in which we operate are of little difference in comparison to corporate and government leaders? This function, this task, cannot be over-emphasized. On it depends any hope of positive movement forward from the weak and ineffective condition in which we find ourselves today.

What about "democratic centralism?"

Since the turn of the century almost 100 years ago and the insistence by Russian revolutionary V.I. Lenin that an organization of "professional revolutionaries" was necessary to make revolution, the most powerful socialist currents internationally have upheld the idea of a centralized, yet democratic, organizational structure as the model necessary to achieve success. In theory, the concept is one which allows for the fullest and widest democratic debate within the organization prior to the point at which a decision is made. At that point, however, all members of the organization, whether in the decision-making majority or the minority, are expected to carry out the decision made fully and wholeheartedly until the point at which the question comes up for review again.

U.S. revolutionary Arthur Kinoy has spoken of how this concept "sets up an inevitable contradiction between these two poles within every democratic-centralist organization. The contradiction can be resolved positively only through the conscious struggle in which neither pole is submerged or destroyed and both are strengthened and unified. Failure to do so can result in serious distortions of the ability of the revolutionary organization to give the leadership required at moments of crisis. . .

"It is within this context that the many distortions in the role and functioning of a 'vanguard party' which developed in this country in the '30s, '40s and '50s must be studied. The failure to conduct a struggle against the distortions of centralism . . . led to the grossest kind of bureaucracy and elitism. . . Without a conscious struggle for full democratic involvement of the base of a revolutionary organization in the shaping of policy, the built-in tendencies toward dictatorial, top-down control take over. . ." (2)

The historical roots of these distortions lie in the reality of Russian society prior to the revolution of 1917 and the concomitant form of organization developed by the Bolshevik Party.

Prior to the February 1917 first Russian revolution, Czarist Russia was a repressive, dictatorial society. In order to survive as an organization Lenin and other Bolshevik leaders structured the revolutionary party in a way which made it difficult for the Czar's secret police to infiltrate and destroy it. A more wide-open, more democratic structure was not possible, and, in any event, there were few democratic traditions from which to draw even if conditions had been less restrictive.

Unfortunately, the centralized Bolshevik model was upheld as the model for other parties elsewhere around the world who were inspired by the Soviet revolution in 1917. And once Lenin died and Stalin eventually gained control of the Party apparatus, this model, more-or-less democratic centralist internally during Lenin's time (although hardly a model of democratic tolerance when it came to other political organizations and parties, including Left political parties), became increasingly bureaucratic centralist and heavily top-down and repressive.

History has demonstrated without a doubt that this distorted form of "democratic centralism" should be confined to the scrap heap of history. But there are other aspects to this structure which should be considered as to their relevance today.

The work of taking on and defeating a powerful, extremely wealthy ruling group involves many things. To the Bolsheviks there were two additional considerations in creating the type of party which they did. One was the need for members who were thoroughly steeled through struggle, tough and able to stand up to the rigors of a long-term battle against autocracy and Czarist repression. It would not do, so the thinking went, to open up the party to those whose level of commitment was lacking, and those who "burned out," slid backwards or grew tired had to be demoted or purged.

There is no question that a revolutionary organization in the U.S. must be made up of people who are committed to working hard and strengthening themselves to be able to "hang in" and "keep the faith" for the long haul. And it is also the case that people do grow tired or have their ideals tempered in negative ways by daily exposure to the dominant and increasingly pervasive corporate culture. Yet the primary method that must be used to help us all stay strong and committed is not internal struggle and purging but, instead, constructive criticism and mutual support. A supportive revolutionary culture is the key to maintaining the levels of dedication and commitment necessary if we are to have a chance of winning.

Secondly, the Bolsheviks made a distinction between the more "advanced," more "class-conscious" workers and those with more limited socialist inclinations. Their strategy was based upon molding the former into a military-style organization in which there was ongoing ideological education and training in the techniques of mass organizing.

In retrospect, it is easy to see how this approach could lead to the elitist, top-down forms and methods of organization which came to characterize those who followed it. When the reality of differences in consciousness and commitment between the most "advanced" and the great mass of workers becomes institutionalized into organizational form, there is a natural separation which, unless consciously recognized, addressed and struggled with, can cause disastrous results.

And why wasn't it "recognized, addressed and struggled with?" In large part it was because of the tremendous economic difficulties faced by the Soviet Union, for close to 30 years the only country attempting to build what was called "socialism," faced with an overwhelmingly peasant, poorly-industrialized economy, and a low level of culture (i.e., a low level of literacy, few democratic traditions, etc.). In these circumstances, it is not surprising that things turned out as badly as they did.

Today, however, is a different reality. Not only are the limitations of the Soviet Bolshevik model understood on a wide scale among activists on the Left; there is a much greater appreciation of the importance of democracy in the functioning of oppositional movements to capitalism.

Samir Amin, writing of conditions in the countries of the South (Latin America, Africa and Asia), has referred to the fact that, "The demand for democracy has indeed assumed proportions never before seen in the countries of the third world: in many countries it has already won the first place in the conscience of the middle classes and is penetrating into the popular, especially urban, strata. This phenomenon is probably new, since until (recently) the demand for democracy has remained limited to particular segments of the urban bourgeoisie and had only been expressed there forcefully at particular moments of radicalization of the anti-imperialist struggles. . . The key feature of the dominant tendencies of the popular and radical movements for national liberation (in the past) was more its progressive social content than the democratic conviction of their militants. . . I do not think I am caricaturing reality in saying that the old peasant-soldier of the Chinese Liberation Army was thinking, as he entered Beijing in 1949, of the agrarian reform, but was ignorant of the meaning of democracy. Today, on this level, his son, worker or student, has new aspirations. . . This is an important and definite advance, which I believe to be irreversible." (3)

This reality in the Third World is <u>certainly</u> the case within the industrialized, "democratic" countries of Europe and North America. Within the United States large numbers of progressive-minded people have stayed away in droves from groups that have a minimal commitment to democracy—many labor unions, many Marxist parties, groups like the once-promising National Rainbow Coalition. Recent history on the Left is a history littered with the remains of failed efforts at building organization, failures in many cases because democracy was given lip-service and not genuine commitment on the part of the leadership.

This set of "material realities" on a world scale and within the United States is an extremely positive development. It means that it is possible, it is on the agenda of history, to build qualitatively different forms of organization, including revolutionary organization. Indeed, this is one of the key questions which must be resolved if we are to have hope for the future. What, concretely, would this mean?

One example comes from Dallas, Texas. There the Bois d'Arc Patriots, an organization based initially in white working-class East Dallas, confronted the problem of how to integrate people at different levels of commitment, ability, skills and available time, and how to do so in a democratic way, while retaining a structure which made it difficult for outside enemies to divide or disrupt it. At the time at which this contradiction was confronted, in the mid-1970s, the Patriots were a semi-revolutionary organization, "a tightly knit group of the most committed people."

"As Patriot causes became more popular, many non-East Dallas, non-poor people began to get interested in helping. These people tended to feel that they lacked input and oftentimes conveyed this to the Patriot Steering Committee. Contradictions surfaced generally among people who viewed the Steering Committee as 'ignorant' and/or 'dictatorial' and felt that the Committee had no authority to tell them how to use their talents. These conflicts resulted in several purges, but had the net effect of causing the Steering Committee to assess the need for such new talent in the context of an improved, more formalized and inclusive structure.

"The conclusions reached were revealing: 1) there was no inherent contradiction between the 'educated' and 'non-educated' members, as evidenced by the fact that the Steering Committee was already composed of both; 2) people who had various bourgeois skills were definitely needed, but a means of subordinating the individual's desires to the organization's needs had to be formalized through structure; 3) this structure would have to involve a mechanism for input, for criticism, for handling grievances, for allowing people to participate and progress at their own pace, relatively; 4) the Steering Committee and the Patriots as well had to develop a more broad based membership in order to consolidate the gains made by the Alliance [the East Dallas Tenants' Alliance, a mass membership organization 'with strong public visibility and broad-based support'], in particular; and 5) a comprehensive political education program focusing on class consciousness in monopoly capitalist society was necessary.

"After several community meetings and much consideration by the Steering Committee, a formal structure was approved. The structure differentiates between supporters and resource people, members of associations or work committees on one hand and members on the other. Membership is further differentiated between those who receive organizational benefits and in return are 'obligated' to assist in community efforts either with their time or money (dues), and those who make a 'commitment.' Supporters are urged to attend, if practical, monthly general meetings which emphasize fellowship (having a covered dish, family night supper type of format) and which are a source of recruitment and solidification. Criticism and self-criticism is encouraged during these meetings. . .

"The structure is basically democratic centralist. The Steering Committee remains in the position to make or approve all policy decisions, based on input and analysis from all levels of membership and affiliation. Blacks and Browns as well as Whites participate on the Steering Committee. Implementation of policy is the responsibility of the various appropriate levels of membership." (4)

I have quoted from this article at length for a number of reasons:

1) The experience of the Patriots is the experience of an indigenous group of working-class people, some of whom were exposed to Marxist ideas but who did <u>not</u> then mechanically set up an organizational structure divorced from the reality of the community they were committed to organizing. This was an authentic, honest effort of working-class revolutionaries in the United States to apply revolutionary theory and experience creatively and non-dogmatically to their conditions.

2) The Patriots consciously dealt with the contradiction between "those who make a 'commitment'" and those who, for whatever reason, can't or won't do so. They came up with organic ways of involving and integrating these people into the work of the organization, which allowed for input by the less-committed into decision-making, while retaining a structure which was relatively secure. After all, they were not exactly popular with the powers-that-be in Dallas, which in fact did make efforts to isolate and destroy them, and they had to take this into account.

3) Their structure "emphasize(d) fellowship (having a covered dish, <u>family night supper</u> [Glick emphasis] type of format)," as well as encouraging "criticism and self-criticism." In other words, their structure integrated <u>community-building</u> into the process of organization-building and activism.

<u>These are all lessons we who wish to build democratic mass organizations, a popular alliance/party uniting those organizations, and a revolutionary organzation committed to helping the alliance grow and succeed, have to learn from.</u>

There is one more key question to answer: <u>how should a new revolutionary organization be built?</u>

There is a need for an identification of those organizers who are hard at work in the vineyards and who understand that the problems we are facing can only be solved through fundamental, systemic change. Some of these individuals are in socialist or revolutionary groups, but many are not. Almost all are active in trade unions, community organizations or single-issue groups. Many of them are involved with one or more of the existing third party groups. Efforts need to be made by those who understand the need for a profoundly different type of new revolutionary organization to connect with each other and begin focused discussions on key questions related to the road ahead in this country.

Organizational consolidation of a consciously revolutionary organization, or an alliance of relatively like-minded revolutionary groups, will take time. It must proceed in close connection with the process of building the mass popular alliance/independent political party. This will help ensure that the forms of revolutionary organization developed, the theoretical perspectives guiding it, and the way in which its members go about their organizing work on a day-to-day basis, are democratic, grounded in reality, humane and effective.

The question of form and structure for a revolutionary organization needs to be one of the important points on the agenda for serious review and discussion prior to any finalization of structure. This review must include an in-depth discussion about the realities of United States society as it pertains to the importance of democracy, as well as the need for security against infiltration and disruption by government agents.

This process of regroupment needs to involve the many tens of thousands of activists who are not presently members of Left political groups. Some of these were formerly members of such groups but left them out of disillusionment with the lack of democracy or other problems. Others are young people whose involvement is essential. Their input and insights will play a critical role in shaping a revolutionary organization capable of fulfilling its historic role.

Footnotes

1) Carl Boggs, The Two Revolutions: Antonio Gramsci and the Dilemmas of Western Marxism, South End Press, p. 23

2) Arthur Kinoy, "Some Further Thoughts on the Road Ahead," published by the Mass Party Organizing Committee, p. 35

3) Samir Amin, "Social Movements in the Periphery," in Transforming the Revolution, Monthly Review Press, p. 128

4) The Bois d'Arc Patriots, "Inner-City Organizing in Dallas," Green Mountain Quarterly, No. 5, February, 1977, p. 33

TACTICS FOR A NEW SOCIETY

"The mode of existence of the new (revolutionary)* can no longer consist of eloquence, the external and momentary arousing of sentiments and passions, but must consist of being actively involved in practical life, as a builder, an organizer, 'permanently persuasive' because he is not purely an orator. . ." (Gramsci, "The Formation of Intellectuals," from The Modern Prince and Other Writings) (1)

And how, exactly, as much as "exactness" can be projected forward, should a popular alliance/party and a new revolutionary organization growing out of and organically connected to it go about its task of building a movement capable of winning political power?

In addressing this "how" question, the question of tactics, we should review the strategic approach we have been developing up to the present. We should not make the error of mistaking tactics for a strategy. Just as form should follow from function, the "how" must follow from the overall plan.

Our strategy consists of the following elements:

1) In order to amass the strength necessary to challenge and overcome the ruling corporate elite, a popular alliance is necessary. This alliance must unite significant sectors of the women's movement, movements of people of color and working class movements, as well as people with disabilities, farmers, senior citizens, gays/lesbians, environmentalists, youth and others on the receiving end of capitalist injustice or oppression.

2) Racism, sexism and homophobia, as well as other destructive ideas and patterns of thought and action, must be actively combated in the course of building the alliance. The right to autonomous organization by people of color, women, or other distinct social groups as they determine is necessary, at the same time that the alliance is built, must be upheld as a central organizational principle.

3) Within the alliance, as well as within each of the sectors or constituences making it up (e.g., the women's movement, labor, people of color, etc.), it is critical that working-class people, particularly working-

---

*In the original the word used is not "revolutionary" but "intellectual," but this was written taking into account the prison censor. "Revolutionary" is certainly appropriate here.

class women, people of color and those from the low-income sector of the working class, be genuinely supported in their efforts to give leadership and actively encouraged to become leaders. Because of the reality of their lives, they have important insights which can increase the chances that the alliance is not derailed or deflected from its mission.

4) The emergence of an independent political party out of and one with the alliance is crucial in the struggle for control of the government, a necessity if the government, the economy, the culture, the society as a whole are to be transformed in a positive, democratic, human-needs-meeting direction. This party will be primarily electoral in nature, running candidates for office at all levels, but it must also have an activist, issue-oriented component to help combat inevitable tendencies toward elitism and bureaucracy on the part of successful candidates for elected office and within the party itself.

5) Forms of organization at a grassroots level must be built which consciously encourage, involve, educate, and develop the leadership of working-class people. Full-scale democracy, mutual support, honest criticism and self-criticism, and basic truthfulness must characterize the way in which the organizations making up the alliance function on a day-to-day basis, as much as is humanly possible.

6) A new revolutionary organization growing out of and integrally connected to all of the above processes can play a valuable role in helping the popular alliance navigate the dangerous currents of political struggle against the ruling class. It must develop an ideology rooted in the realities of U.S. history and society, an organizational structure at once fully democratic, effective, actively anti-bureaucratic and open to change as conditions change, and an internal process which builds community and supports its members at the same time that it goes about its work in a coherent way.

With this as the essence of our strategy, what are some of the ways to go about implementing it?

First, possibly the most important, is a new way of working with and relating to those we interact with on a daily basis. This may sound trite, but it isn't. Gramsci is quoted at the beginning of this section talking about the limitations of "eloquence" and the necessity of "being actively involved in practical life as a builder, an organizer." Builders and organizers function differently than eloquent speakers. Of necessity, they must be more humble, more collective in their way of working with others, consciously encouraging others to grow and learn. To build, they must have a vision of what it is they wish to construct, and this needs to be communicated to others to motivate them. This is not the same thing as getting up on the stage and speaking, the "momentary arousing of sentiments and passions."

Immanuel Wallerstein has spoken of this different way of working in relationship to the building of unity among various anti-systemic movements. He speaks of the need for "a conscious effort at empathetic understanding of the other movements, their histories, their priorities, their social bases, their current concerns. Correspondingly, increased empathy needs to be accompanied by restraint in rhetoric. It does not mean that movements should not be frank with each other, even in public. It means that the discussion needs to be self-consciously comradely, based on the recognition of a unifying objective, a relatively democratic, relatively egalitarian world.

"Consequently, this means that the movements will have to devote considerably more energy than has historically been the case to intermovement diplomacy. To the extent that the movements come to internalize the sense that the social transformation they are seeking will not occur in a single apocalpytic moment, but as a continuous process, one continually hard-fought, they may learn to concentrate their energies somewhat less exclusively on the immediate tactics of change and somewhat more on constructing middle-run stepping-stones. In such a context, intramovement diplomacy becomes a very useful expenditure of energy. It will make possible the combination of daring leaps and structural consolidation which could make plausible a progressive transformation of the world-system." (2)

Wallerstein raises another important point for consideration here when he talks of "social transformation... not occur(ing) in a single apocalyptic moment."

For understandable reasons, traditional Marxist or other revolutionary groups have projected that the struggle for state power, for control of the instruments of government, is the central objective. Without the accomplishment of this objective, it will not be possible to fully implement a revolutionary agenda of social and economic transformation. This continues to be valid today, yet at the same time history has shown that the "single apocalyptic moment" of taking power, alone, is no guarantee that the types of changes hoped for will actually come to pass. Indeed, it is the case that the key to taking power, holding it and, then, transforming

-84-

and decentralizing it, will depend upon the many other things that must go with that work, that objective.

What, concretely, are those "many other things?"

One thing is certainly changes in consciousness, a new way of seeing and understanding the world. Without question this is an absolute necessity on the part of large numbers of people, not necessarily a majority, but certainly a significant minority, prior to the winning of control of government. Among this minority there will of course be unevenness in the extent of a changed consciousness, but, at a minimum, there must be a clear recognition by all that the problems we are facing are systemic, resolvable only by a new, truly democratic form of government, with steps taken to end the domination by massive corporations of economic life and government, and with a more cooperative, people-oriented approach to decision-making and human interaction throughout all institutions of society.

It is realistic to expect that in a number of local areas, possibly a large number, genuinely progressive, independent, "people before profits" governments could emerge prior to the "big change." There will be major limitations on what they can accomplish absent change in the national government and an end to economic domination by corporate America, but, at a minimum, they can place themselves on the side of the popular alliance and the working class in its various struggles for justice and change, and help to advance political consciousness. They can also ameliorate some of the worst effects of capitalism on people and the environment through legal powers and political pressure.

To a limited extent some small-scale economic alternatives can develop such as employee-owned and -controlled enterprises and cooperatives. In addition to the economic benefits accruing to their members, they can also serve as a base for the development of the alliance, as well as for changes in consciousness.

Within the educational system, public as well as some private institutions, there is already a progressive current made up of parents, teachers, some students and some administrators. The same is true within the health care system. In neither case are progressive ideas dominant, as witness the debacle in 1994 during the national debate on health care, but these are movements which are not going to go away.

Within the established church and organized religion, there are large numbers of believers who oppose racism, sexism and homophobia, support efforts for economic and social justice, are concerned about the effect of transnational corporate power in the world, and would be involved with a popular alliance.

And there are certainly other forms of organization within "civil society"—labor unions, community and environmental organizations, community associations, cultural groups—which either are or can become politically progressive.

However, in the absence of a popular alliance and a revolutionary organization committed to the alliance, these various strands of hope are very limited in their impacts. Even more, they are limited in their ability to <u>envision</u> something different replacing the current political/economic structures. They tend to be essentially reformist in their political outlook, usually unwilling to challenge the dominant powers-that-be too directly because of concern about losing the possibility of access. But collectively, they have the potential to play a crucial role in both developing the beginnings of alternatives to the existing system and strengthening the popular alliance movement in its long march, its "war of position" (Gramsci) toward the winning of control of the government.

Internationalism, the forging of links between working-class people in the United States and workers in other parts of the world, is clearly a critical necessity. In this time of NAFTA, GATT and the WTO, when the dominant supra-national financial and corporate power elite are on the offensive for every possible profit-making advantage, it is hard to see how we can succeed in our objectives unless there are strengthened labor and popular movements in those countries being penetrated by capital to an even greater extent than in the past. The living standards and working conditions of the peoples of Central and South America, Africa and Asia must be raised, which can only happen through a combination of more effective organization by the workers and peasants of those parts of the world and international solidarity on the part of those living in the United States, Western Europe, Japan and elsewhere. The U.S. trade union movement must reverse direction, going from past AFL-CIO collaboration with the CIA to genuine efforts to work in a cooperative and respectful way with other struggling unions around the world.

And what about labor? For large sections of the Left, for many decades, trade unions have been seen as a strategically key arena, for understandable reasons, given the fact that they have been the primary form of working- class organization.

Saul Alinsky has written of how, "throughout Western civilization, radicals tied their destiny to the organized labor movement. To them the labor movement was the key to the door of the future world of economic justice and the social betterment of mankind. The labor movement has been as much of an ideological foundation to all left-wing thinkers as the Ten Commandments and the Golden Rule are to devout religionists. . .

"In recent times [the late 60s] it has become increasingly clear that the organized labor movement as it is constituted today (emphasis in original) is as much a concomitant of a capitalist economy as is capital. Organized labor is predicated upon the basic premise of collective bargaining between employers and employees. This premise can obtain only in an employer-employee type of society. If the labor movement is to maintain its own identity and security, it must of necessity protect that kind of society. . .

"As labor unions have become strong, wealthy, fat and respectable, they have behaved more and more like organized business. In many cases their courses have run so parallel that in a basic sense organized labor has become a partner of organized business." (3)

Has this situation changed since Alinsky wrote these words? Yes and no. There are individual national unions, particularly the United Electrical Workers Union, the Teamsters, the Oil, Chemical and Atomic Workers Union, the United Mineworkers and the west coast Longshoremen's Union which, as this is written, are about something different, and there are certainly many local unions and some regional divisions of national unions that are also. Most of these unions have joined together to form and build the U.S. Labor Party, an extremely important development for the labor movement. But for the dominant, national leadership of the AFL-CIO unions, Alinsky's critique still tends to be true.

One fairly recent example is the shabby treatment accorded the locked-out workers at the A.E. Staley corn-sweetener factory in Decatur, Illinois by the then-newly-elected AFL-CIO national leadership.

In October 1995, a national AFL-CIO convention in New York City elected a new slate of leaders, led by John Sweeney, former President of the Service Employees International Union. At the national convention in New York City where the election took place, a pledge of support was made by the new leadership to assist those Staley workers who had been locked out for over two years. Yet, despite the promise of resources to be put into a "Boycott Pepsi" campaign, as a way of getting Pepsi to cancel its corn sweetener contract with Staley and put pressure on Staley to negotiate in good faith with the locked-out workers, nothing was ever done. Largely as a result, Staley eventually forced the local union to accept a terrible settlement on its terms.

This does not mean that we should ignore or downgrade trade union organizing. Despite all their weaknesses, unions continue to be a key arena for organizing working-class people both for survival and towards a different type of social/economic arrangement. We should not, however, hold up the trade union movement as the key sector of the popular alliance upon which all else must either move forward or wait. History has proven convincingly, with many examples, that this approach is wrong.

Kim Moody, a keen observer of the trade unions for many years, has written of the need for "a multi-organizational model to take advantage of the complex ways in which capital has centralized its socialization of the working class. Not only trade unions, but political organizations and parties, women's and ethnic class-based organizations, and community-based labor organizations will be needed to provide a unifying 'home' for the diverse elements of tomorrow's working class movement. . .

"The model we should promote is not so much the social democratic model of Europe (trade unions plus party) as that of Latin America (and South Africa) where unions, parties, and mass urban community-based organizations (frequently led by women) increasingly function as arms of a single working-class movement." (4)

Another reason for the type of flexibility in organizational form that Moody argues for is the changing nature of the workforce brought on by changes in the nature and organization of work. The U.S. workforce is increasingly characterized by a growing number of part-time, temporary or contract jobs with no, or few, health care, pension or other benefits. Over half of all new jobs being created fall into this category, and close to 1/3 of the entire workforce.

This is no small piece of business—almost one-third of the workforce in insecure, usually low-paying, no-benefits, high-turnover occupations! This is not a sector of the workforce that will be easy to organize into the traditional trade union form of organization.

One important alternative form of organization is community-based workers centers. This form of organization is growing, particularly within communities of color, as committed activists of color attempt to deal with both the racism within much of the trade union structure and the needs of the people in those communities. Many of the people they work with are unemployed, and others have the kind of insecure jobs that are increasingly the only ones available within this capitalist economy. Through these centers forms of organization are created which link both workers' oppression on the job and their survival and human needs as members of the community. It is an organizational form that almost certainly will continue to grow and develop. It is an example of the kind of flexibility in organizational form necessary to be responsive to the needs of the working class.

There is another new sector of the working class, so-called "knowledge workers." What is their importance, or potential importance, in relationship to the strategy and tactics we are discussing here?

Jerry Harris and Carl Davidson have spoken to this issue in an article, "The Cybernetic Revolution and the Crisis of Capitalism." They write there about how "the application of knowledge is now the primary means of new value production" for individual capitalists and the system as a whole. "The application of micro-electronics technology has already increased computer productivity by one million. Intellectual capital, developed and held by knowledge workers and encoded in software and smart machines, is the key element of wealth in today's information capitalism. . .

"In America there are two growing class strata that need close attention. These are the new knowledge workers and the rapidly expanding contingent labor force. . . Knowledge workers today are in the position of the old industrial proletariat. They are key to the enhanced production of surplus value. Just as blue collar workers contained two sides—the conservative labor aristocracy as well as the most progressive sector of labor supportive of democracy and socialism—knowledge workers will be divided into two as well. One sector will form the social base for the defense of information capitalism regardless of its excesses. Others will deeply understand the potential the new technology has for creating and sustaining a new social order. This progressive side also is born from the conditions of its own labor. . . The economic organization of knowledge workers emphasizes less hierarchy, less bureaucracy, more information about and control of the job process, and greater participation or empowerment at the site of work. This lays the basis for socialist norms of labor, and blurs lines between mental and manual work, which is the historic division between management and employee. The political voice of this strata has already emerged in today's battles for democratic use and control of information technologies." (5)

According to Harris and Davidson, it is estimated that the "knowledge worker" sector of the workforce will soon reach 20% of the total workforce. In numerical terms alone, this is clearly a sector which cannot be ignored.

This is also the most highly-paid sector of the working class, more a "middle class" in popular terminology, and this will mean less of a willingness, in general, to engage in militant action on behalf of social change. This is logical. When people earn enough money to own a home, more than one car, a children's college bank account, or the like, they cannot be expected to put themselves on the line in the same way that someone who is barely making it might be willing to do. When there's a lot to lose, there's more soul-searching necessary for most people before they are willing to take action which might risk losing it.

This does not mean Harris and Davidsons' arguments are invalid about the importance of this sector of the workforce. Their concerns—"ecology, disarmament, peace and human rights issues, and expanded access to information and education"—are also issues very much on the agenda of the popular alliance. They have to be part of the overall program the alliance is working on both now and in the future when power is achieved. But there are limitations on the part of this sector when it comes to stronger forms of action; this has to be taken into account when devising appropriate tactics.

Political activists, organizations and movements always have to consider the political effects of the ways in which they struggle. If you are trying to reach the hearts and minds of others, you can't act stupid and self-righteous about the demands you are trying to advance; people will turn you off. There is a mass media which usually has to be considered when determining the forms of struggle and the tactics used. Sometimes the reaction of the police may be a consideration.

Our tactics must proceed from an understanding of certain basic realities about the U.S. population, particularly the working class. One is its low level of political consciousness. This is reflective of and reinforced by the fragmentation of independent, grassroots groups and the absence of a visible progressive alternative to the Democrats and Republicans, not to mention deep-seated racism and other divisive ideologies.

Because of this reality, we need to consciously use tactics which allow us to educate and interact directly with working-class and other people as we go about our organizing, with as little room given for distortion of our ideas as possible. What does this mean concretely? It might mean, for example, that instead of gearing a campaign around an issue toward the mass media, the campaign would first be focused towards a massive, grassroots outreach campaign, or with media that is definitely friendly. Not that the media would not and should not be considered and worked with to elicit the best possible coverage, but in the absence of serious efforts to directly transmit our message to the people we are trying to reach, serious distortions are likely to occur.

Another example is the growing use of fasting and hunger strikes in various parts of the country around a number of different issues: the U.S. war on Nicaragua, the counter-Columbus Day movement, local student struggles, cuts in food and welfare programs for low-income people, even labor organizing campaigns. This tactic has significance in several ways.

First, it is difficult to question the sincerity of those going without food for days. Even if you disagree with them, there is usually a grudging respect for their willingness to sacrifice for what they believe in, and for many people this makes a difference in their ability to think soberly about what is being attempted through the action.

Second, fasting communicates seriousness and urgency without the use of violence. It is the antithesis of the caricature of the "terrorist," the revolutionary with no concern for human life, the evil, scheming "communist," and part of our work has to be the breaking down of those caricatures and stereotypes. Fasting is one, although not the only, way to do that.

Non-violent civil disobedience is another tactic that, as we have recently seen in Seattle, Wa. in November, 1999 and Washington, D.C. in April, 2000, can "push the envelope" in a way which aims a bright spotlight onto the issues being raised and educates widely. Indeed, as this is written, there are signs that a non-violent "army" is emerging in the United States, one deeply committed to egalitarian, democratic, creative, joyous yet militant direct action in support of global justice and environmental sustainability. This is a profoundly important development.

What about the question of "armed struggle?" For some revolutionary Marxists, this is almost a litmus test as to whether or not one is, indeed, sufficiently revolutionary. Should this tactic be automatically ruled out or counted in when it comes to the U.S. struggle for political power?

It is difficult to see "armed struggle" as having much relevance to United States realities as we begin the 21st century. Our primary work is ideological and political, the development of grassroots-based organization and alliances that can raise the level of understanding on the part of the working class and sectors of the middle class as to the <u>reasons for</u> their problems and <u>the way out</u>, the <u>realistic possibility</u> of a way out if we can transcend the competitiveness, the racism, sexism and the like which are holding us back from united struggle against our common enemy.

In this work, basic, mass organizational tactics will be the bedrock of our approach: leafletting, petitioning and door-to-door campaigns on relevant issues, mass meetings and demonstrations, sit-ins, fasting and civil disobedience when necessary, voter registration and the running of candidates for political office, and other more creative ways of reaching out and applying pressure around our demands. As a unified alliance emerges, taking the form of a mass political party, there may well be the potential for the use of a tactic rarely used in U.S. history, the general strike, paralyzing the economy through mass non-participation.

At the same time, this process of building up our strength and unity on the road to political power will not go unopposed. The corporate and financial rulers will apply pressure for the use of the FBI, CIA, police, reactionary right-wing groups and even the armed forces, if necessary, to disrupt, divide and repress a growing movement. Based on recent history during the '60s and early '70s, it is to be expected that this repression will come down harder on activists from communities of color than on those from the European-American community. It would not be surprising if there were some "armed struggle" in reaction against some of the agents of repression, particularly the police. If this does happen, it is the responsibility of those committed to the alliance to support those on the receiving end of police violence and to pinpoint the source of the problem: government/corporate injustice and/or repressive government action in support of unjust policies and structures. It will also be necessary to counter the efforts of government to portray the alliance as a violent group.

Of course, it is possible that conditions within the United States may change. Although it is wrong to <u>count on</u> this happening, it is a distinct possibility that there may be a major financial crisis of the debt-ridden capitalist system, leading to a serious economic decline. This could lead to a much more repressive set of measures by a desperate ruling class, and this in turn may make the question of "armed struggle" much more relevant than it is now or is likely to be in the near future.

The best defense against this reality coming to pass is what we do today. German theologian and anti-Nazi resistance activist Dietrich Bonhoeffer once said, "Real generosity toward the future lies in giving all to the present." Elsewhere he said, while imprisoned in a Nazi prison camp during World War II prior to his execution, "There remains for us only the very narrow way, often extremely difficult to find, of living every day as if it were our last, and yet living in faith and responsibility as though there were to be a great future. . . It may be that the day of judgment will dawn tomorrow, and in that case, though not before, we shall gladly stop working for a better future." (6)

Our conditions within the United States are not the conditions of Nazi Germany, but Bonhoeffer's words still ring true. There is an urgent, compelling need for people in the United States to take seriously their responsibilities to themselves and to others. People are needed who are willing to study our realities and work to change them, in cooperation with a growing movement of like-minded sisters and brothers. There is no other, more important calling today. The world needs U.S. revolutionaries of a new type, new women and new men who have learned from history and are able to move forward together at a qualitatively higher level because of it.

We need a new revolutionary movement and forms of organization that are efficient in all of the traditional ways that people think of effective organization. To win, however, we must also build new people, constantly; create organizations and an alliance/party that keeps people honest and growing all the time; and reach outwards to incorporate more and more people in this process, in concentric circles. Let's take this time of crisis and turn it into the historic opportunity it also provides. The need is very great.

Footnotes

1) Antonio Gramsci, "The Formation of Intellectuals," from The Modern Prince and Other Writings, International Publishers, p. 122

2) Immanual Wallerstein, "Antisystemic Movements," in Transforming the Revolution, Monthly Review Press, p. 52

3) Saul Alinsky, Reveille for Radicals, Vintage Books, pps. 24 and 27

4) Kim Moody, "Pulled Apart, Pushed Together: The North American Working Class," from Crossroads Magazine, October, 1994, p. 10

5) Harris and Davidson, "The Cybernetic Revolution and the Crisis of Capitalism," from cy.Rev, July, 1994, pps. 6, 10 and 11

6) Dietrich Bonhoeffer, Letters and Papers from Prison, Fontana Books, pps. 146-147